THE DYNAMIC POWER
OF OBEDIENCE

THE DYNAMIC POWER OF OBEDIENCE

AN ESSENTIAL CHRISTIAN PRACTICE FOR BEARING FRUIT

A.W. TOZER

COMPILED AND EDITED BY JAMES L. SNYDER

BETHANYHOUSE

a division of Baker Publishing Group
Minneapolis, Minnesota

© 2025 by International Literary Properties, LLC

Published by Bethany House Publishers
Minneapolis, Minnesota
BethanyHouse.com

Bethany House Publishers is a division of
Baker Publishing Group, Grand Rapids, Michigan

Printed in the United States of America

ISBN 9780764244773 (paper)
ISBN 9780764245138 (casebound)
ISBN 9781493450916 (ebook)

Library of Congress Cataloging-in-Publication Control Number: 2024054643

Scripture quotations are from the King James Version of the Bible.

Cover design by InsideOut Creative Arts, Inc.

James L. Snyder is represented by The Steve Laube Agency.

Baker Publishing Group publications use paper produced from sustainable forestry practices and postconsumer waste whenever possible.

25 26 27 28 29 30 31   7 6 5 4 3 2 1

CONTENTS

INTRODUCTION

While putting this book together, I was reminded of how much the concept and question of obedience has been a part of my life. As a child, my parents expected obedience in every sense of the word. I thought going to school might be different, but the teachers and faculty expected absolute obedience from me as well.

When I graduated from high school, I got a job and experienced the same thing. My employer expected obedience from me every day that I worked there, and if I didn't obey, it jeopardized my employment.

Obedience is a central part of the Christian experience, but the key to this obedience is submitting to the authority of the Lord Jesus Christ. I must surrender completely to Christ without compromise even though oftentimes my obedience will be shrouded in confusion. While I may not understand the reason for obedience in a particular situation, this should never affect my surrender to God's will.

My obedience will be constantly challenged, just like Adam and Eve were challenged by the serpent in the Garden of Eden. God gave the couple but one command to obey: do not eat the fruit of the tree of the knowledge of good and evil.

When Adam and Eve disobeyed, they lost their identity in God (Genesis 3). This has seeped into all of humanity. Beginning with Adam and Eve and continuing to this day, the world has been deceived by the enemy of God, all of us caught up in a habitual disobedience.

Later, in Genesis 22, the question of obedience comes to a head with Abraham, whom God calls on to sacrifice his son Isaac on the altar. Here, Abraham doesn't attempt to negotiate with God; he would be either all in or not in at all. The fact that Abraham obeyed God tells us a little bit about his relationship with Him, for he was willing to slay his own son in obedience to God's command.

In this book, Tozer outlines the spiritual vows crucial to obedience. He points out that this is not a one-time decision but a lifetime commitment. I don't know what I will be like ten years from now, but if I'm still living, I'll need to continue to make obedient choices day by day. Such obedience to God and His Word is not selective and must be done in the right spirit.

When I'm committed to a life of obedience that is non-negotiable, I'll discover a power in my Christian life I didn't know before and can't explain now. Obedience will cost me everything, but it will also give me everything God has in store for me.

The Dynamic Power of Obedience covers several aspects of obedience, although it's not drawn from a single series of Tozer sermons on the topic; rather, it's built on a variety of sermons taken from many different series that emphasized obedience throughout the life of the Christian.

God doesn't force us to obey His commands, just as He didn't force Adam and Eve to obey His command not to eat of the forbidden fruit. Obedience is our way of loving, honoring, and worshiping God through our individual choices.

I especially appreciate this quote from Tozer: "The obedient Christian cannot die until his work is finished." He's referring to those followers of Christ who are committed to moment-by-moment obedience to the Holy Spirit. For if we follow this path, our obedience will carry us through all of life's trials and tribulations and get us to where God wants us to be.

I'm confident that if A. W. Tozer were alive today, he would be very pleased if this book helped to encourage you and me in our walk with God as we endeavor to obey Him faithfully in all things.

Dr. James L. Snyder

1

The Sacred Goal of Obedience

*Thou art worthy, O Lord, to receive glory and honour
and power: for thou hast created all things, and for thy
pleasure they are and were created.*

Revelation 4:11

Since becoming a Christian, I've thought a lot about the subject and discipline of obedience. If I'm to understand what it means to be a Christian, I need to understand obedience. And if I'm to understand obedience, I need to understand Christianity as a whole. When these two come together, it is life-changing for the believer.

Let us go back to the very beginning—Genesis, chapter 1, which of course opens with, "In the beginning God . . ." Let's consider this idea that God was in the beginning; moreover, He was *before* the beginning. This is one of the most important concepts in the Bible, and yet we will never understand it for as long as we live.

Later, in Genesis 1:26–27, we read another essential aspect of creation:

> And God said, Let us make man in our image, after our likeness: and let them have dominion over the fish of the sea, and over the fowl of the air, and over the cattle, and over all the earth, and over every creeping thing that creepeth upon the earth. So God created man in his own image, in the image of God created he him; male and female created he them.

We were created in God's image and after God's likeness. Unlike any other of God's created beings, mankind stands above them all and has dominion over all. "And God blessed them, and God said unto them, Be fruitful, and multiply, and replenish the earth, and subdue it: and have dominion over the fish of the sea, and over the fowl of the air, and over every living thing that moveth upon the earth" (Genesis 1:28).

I find most people, even some Christians, view the creation narrative through human eyes—that is, we try to understand and explain it from a human point of view. But when we do so, we take away from God what rightfully belongs to Him.

Thus when considering the story of creation, we must ask ourselves, *What was God's purpose?* The purpose of all of creation was to give pleasure to God. And the greatest pleasure for Him comes from mankind, which He created in His own image and after His own likeness. His creation gave Him pleasure because it was "good."

It is sometimes hard for me to comprehend that God found pleasure in His creative work. God made things that He loved, and He loved what He made.

Down through the years, beginning in the Garden of Eden, Satan has twisted aspects of that creation into something that offends God. Satan's goal from the beginning was to take from God that pleasure which rightfully belongs to Him. We see Satan's tactics in Isaiah 14:12–14:

> How art thou fallen from heaven, O Lucifer, son of the morning! how art thou cut down to the ground, which didst weaken the nations! For thou hast said in thine heart, I will ascend into heaven, I will exalt my throne above the stars of God: I will sit also upon the mount of the congregation, in the sides of the north: I will ascend above the heights of the clouds; I will be like the most High.

I think it can rightly be said that this "Lucifer, son of the morning" hates mankind with a hatred rooted in hell. Seeing how God was pleased with mankind, Satan wanted to take that pleasure away from God for himself.

I can only imagine what it was like in the Garden of Eden when there was no sin or depravity. There was nothing to fear there. God had declared His creation of man to be good, which means that, seen through God's eyes, it pleased Him above all else.

Once Adam was released into the Garden of Eden, he was free to do almost anything he wanted. Yet God gave him one command—just one. Adam had access to everything in the garden, that is, except "the tree of the knowledge of good and evil." Genesis 2:16–17 says,

> And the LORD God commanded the man, saying, Of every tree of the garden thou mayest freely eat: But of the tree of

the knowledge of good and evil, thou shalt not eat of it: for in the day that thou eatest thereof thou shalt surely die.

The next thing God did for Adam was to give him "a help," and Adam called her Eve. Like a good husband, Adam explained to Eve what God's one command was and then warned her to avoid the forbidden tree and its fruit. And for some time, she did. We don't know for how long.

But then one day Eve met the "serpent." Interestingly, she wasn't fearful of this serpent because there was no fear present in her or the Garden of Eden at that point. Of all the topics the serpent might have brought up with her, he zeroed in on the one tree she and Adam were not to eat from. That single command from God was the focus of the serpent's attack on Eve.

In Genesis 3:1–5, we read:

Now the serpent was more subtil than any beast of the field which the LORD God had made. And he said unto the woman, Yea, hath God said, Ye shall not eat of every tree of the garden? And the woman said unto the serpent, We may eat of the fruit of the trees of the garden: But of the fruit of the tree which is in the midst of the garden, God hath said, Ye shall not eat of it, neither shall ye touch it, lest ye die. And the serpent said unto the woman, Ye shall not surely die: For God doth know that in the day ye eat thereof, then your eyes shall be opened, and ye shall be as gods, knowing good and evil.

Here, the serpent challenged God's command, suggesting that God was actually lying to Adam and Eve. "Ye shall not surely die" was his claim. The serpent went on to explain that God was fearful of them because if they did eat the fruit of that tree, their eyes would be opened.

I'm sure Satan hated it when God walked with Adam and Eve in the cool of the day, looking on with envy as God found pleasure in Adam and Eve. Satan despised the pleasure mankind brought to God and wanted that pleasure for himself.

So the one command God gave them became the focus of his devious attack. And just one act of disobedience by Adam and Eve brought about the depravity of all mankind, which continues to this very day.

If we are to understand the effects of disobedience, we must understand the full meaning of obedience. What's more, to understand obedience we must come to understand who we are in God's eyes—not who we think we are.

Again, God never forces obedience on anybody because it gives Him pleasure to allow everyone to choose for themselves. He delights in our obedience, and that delight would be negated if we didn't obey Him willingly of our own volition.

Throughout the Scriptures we learn that every choice brings with it a consequence. Every act of obedience opens a door to our growing closer to God, just as every act of disobedience closes a door, further separating us from God.

Each individual's situation and relationship with God is a direct result of their personal obedience or disobedience. This could be what David was meditating on when he wrote, "And he gave them their request; but sent leanness into their soul" (Psalm 106:15).

The consequence of Adam and Eve's sinful choice in the Garden of God was death. This was not only a physical death

15

as we think of it now, but rather the death of something inside them. It was also a spiritual death that came between them and God, separating them from Him.

Up until this time, Adam and Eve walked with God in the cool of the day, and we never see anything after that of God walking with them. They paid for their disobedience with a loss of intimacy with God. I'm sure Adam and Eve missed that fellowship with God in the cool of the day and came to regret their actions.

Yet the consequences were physical as well because God did not create Adam and Eve to die. They were meant to live forever. This disobedience brought death to all humanity. We won't know or understand what living forever was supposed to be like until we die physically and go to heaven.

I can hardly imagine what Adam thought after he had disobeyed. Nor can I imagine what he thought when his son Cain murdered his brother Abel. I wonder how much of that he blamed on himself. Disobedience carries with it a heavy price tag.

Adam and Eve didn't rob a bank, they didn't murder anybody, and they didn't do any of the other hateful things we see in the world today. They just disobeyed a single commandment of God.

Joshua raised the importance of obedience to the people of Israel when he said, "And if it seem evil unto you to serve the Lord, choose you this day whom ye will serve; whether the gods which your fathers served that were on the other side of the flood, or the gods of the Amorites, in whose land ye dwell: but as for me and my house, we will serve the Lord" (Joshua 24:15).

Joshua understood that we give God pleasure when we choose to serve Him. As is pointed out in Joshua 24, we are all given a choice: we can either choose God or we can choose the world.

The apostle Paul knew well the dynamics of obedience and disobedience when he wrote, "For as by one man's disobedience many were made sinners, so by the obedience of one shall many be made righteous" (Romans 5:19).

On the cross, Jesus, because of His great sacrifice, made reconciliation for Adam and Eve's act of disobedience.

The divine purpose of obedience is to bring pleasure to God. God did not create man to stumble around on his own. He created man for himself, and some of the pleasure He got from man was taken away from Him with Adam and Eve's disobedience.

Their disobedience resulted in untold damage, but amidst all that disobedience, God sent His Son into the world to undo it and make all things new again. Now, when we put our faith and trust in Christ and obey His Word, we are called children of God, and our communion with Him is restored.

Christ paid for the disobedience of Adam and Eve, but Satan will pay for his own disobedience. "Then shall he say also unto them on the left hand, Depart from me, ye cursed, into everlasting fire, prepared for the devil and his angels" (Matthew 25:41).

Christ's obedience and sacrifice that led Him to the cross of Calvary undid Adam and Eve's disobedience in the Garden of Eden. God's solution for all disobedience is obedience.

O God, I seek to please Thee in every way. I commit to obey You in all things regardless of the cost to me personally. May Your pleasure be the focus of my life, today and always. Amen.

Trust and Obey

When we walk with the Lord
in the light of his word,
what a glory he sheds on our way!
While we do his good will,
he abides with us still,
and with all who will trust and obey.

Trust and obey, for there's no other way
to be happy in Jesus, but to trust and obey.

Not a burden we bear,
not a sorrow we share,
but our toil he doth richly repay;
not a grief or a loss,
not a frown or a cross,
but is blest if we trust and obey.

But we never can prove
the delights of his love
until all on the altar we lay;
for the favor he shows,
for the joy he bestows,
are for them who will trust and obey.

Then in fellowship sweet
we will sit at his feet,
or we'll walk by his side in the way;
what he says we will do,
where he sends we will go;
never fear, only trust and obey.

John H. Sammis

2

The Church and Obedience

But seek ye first the kingdom of God, and his righteousness; and all these things shall be added unto you.

Matthew 6:33

I want to be frank about the Church's weaknesses and needs, but I know how much injury is done by a sour and critical spirit. I'd rather die now than turn sour. But I also know that the shortest way to the cemetery for any church is to assume that everything is all right and should be left alone. So I want to appraise the situation and report what can be done and what I hope all churches will do.

I look to the Lord Jesus Christ and His servant Paul in this, for they both first appraised and talked about the positive things they saw, then about the negative and what could be done about it. I think that's a perfect pattern for us to follow.

What's right with us, what's wrong with us, and what's best to be done to correct the wrong. I believe that is the most logical, sensible, and reasonable way to approach the Church and the subject of obedience, and so I'll follow this path alongside Christ and Paul.

Some churches are theologically sound, and their emphasis rests in the right place. But even if they're doing such things right, that doesn't necessarily mean they're living out their faith.

Obedience reveals what we truly believe, and in many churches, as I said, the emphasis is indeed in the right place. They are teaching orthodox lessons in their churches, and if you asked them about their beliefs, they would give you all the correct answers. But are they living out what they preach?

Truth be told, some are and some aren't. I believe, in some measure, we are enjoying the presence of God, and this to me is the test of any church. When the presence of the Lord is felt, worship is delightful and heals the hurting soul.

You go out of a church like that quite different from when you went in. You sense the presence of God in the midst of the congregation. You're blessed by the prayer, the worship, and the fellowship. You're drawn to the place because the presence of God and His love are evident there. Lastly, you have a sense of being spiritually tied to the other congregants in the church.

But now let me share some of my concerns, and here again I look to the Lord Jesus Christ and to Paul. I'll point out what I see as deficiencies and then recommend possible remedies. For we need to know what our deficiencies are before we can determine what the remedy or remedies might be in bringing about change.

It seems to me that danger comes to a church when that church has reached a certain ecclesiastical maturity. Young churches just starting out are typically more spiritual, mostly because they must trust God more than the older churches.

There's something wonderful and refreshing about a new church, where everybody seems to love everybody else. The people in a new church tend to be optimistic too, even though they're small and struggling to continue on as they face the many obstacles before them—all while depending on God for His help and guidance. And they encourage each other toward obedience to the Scriptures.

Then time goes on, "success" follows, and churches can become critical or complacent or both. The little, struggling church, so dependent on God in the beginning, slowly and by degrees starts to be less so. The numbers grow, as does the money being collected each week, until soon they're feeling quite comfortable and satisfied with themselves. Eventually, out goes the commitment to obedience to God and His Word.

The freshness, wonder, and enthusiasm that were there among them when the church was small and struggling have gone by the wayside. At first, everything and everybody that came through the door was welcomed and loved, but after some time the people began to care about what others might think.

This is evidence of the cooling of the first love, which our Lord Jesus refers to when He said, "Nevertheless I have somewhat against thee, because thou hast left thy first love" (Revelation 2:4). This means you no longer have the love for the Lord that you once did.

How can it be that we love God less than we once did? If this is the case, there needs to come humility, repentance, and a sincere seeking after God. Obedience goes a long way in restoring our first love.

Another thing that established churches often do is to pull back on their sympathy toward others outside the church community. The danger here is that we find so many things to pray for and busy ourselves with in our fellowship with one another, that this uses up the majority of our time. The result is that we have only a little time left over to pray for and serve those ones outside the church. Thus the focus shifts to being on us and our own pressing needs.

When Job prayed for his friends, God blessed him and doubled everything he had. He was praying outside his own needs, and God honored this. I pray that we might be delivered from holding back our sympathy toward others who are not members of our community.

Praying for, laboring with, and serving the people in our fellowship are certainly necessary, but we must not limit our prayers and service to internal, self-focused needs and concerns. We want to have a growing and thriving church, but only so that we might have a more extensive outreach and Christian influence on the world.

When you get on your knees before the Lord, sometimes it's good not to pray for yourself at all, not to pray for your church at all either, but to pray for others outside the church—praying for these people by name and asking God to give you a heart as big as His heart, asking Him to give you His sympathy and understanding, so that you will love the ones He loves for the same reason.

Sometimes those reasons are not known to us, and sometimes there are no reasons except that God loves them, and we should too. Loving those God loves and looking outside yourself and your needs is an act of obedience that not all churches and Christians have learned to practice. It's essential that we have God's heart for others, not just those within our church family or circle of friends.

Another disadvantage of the larger, successful church can be a lack of care for the lost. Too often we care more for each other, those who already know the Lord, and pray about all the little things that trouble us. In fact, there are many things for which we pray that we don't need to pray for at all.

Meanwhile, we neglect to pray for those who don't yet know Him. Jesus said, "But seek ye first the kingdom of God, and his righteousness; and all these things shall be added unto you"(Matthew 6:33). His words include a command, and they deserve our obedience.

There was a man named John, and he prayed for his friend and his physical health. Being the man of God that he was, he made that prayer one of the most all-embracing and comprehensive prayers possible. He said, "Beloved, I wish above all things that thou mayest prosper and be in health, even as thy soul prospereth" (3 John 1:2). Notice that he didn't just focus on his physical health, but on his soul as well.

Sometimes we pray for people and tell God about the medical reports, but the Lord knows more about this than the doctors. We need to escape from all that and pray that God blesses them physically as much as He blesses them spiritually, so that both their physical and spiritual states will be strong and in good health.

Now let us apply all of this to our obedience to the Lord, as our prayers and actions should always harmonize with God's will. If we humble ourselves and commit to obedience to His Word no matter the cost, we can be assured that the

Holy Spirit will make it abundantly clear those things God wants us to focus on, the people we need to be praying for, and all the rest. Because if our churches are to thrive, they must make the task of obeying God a top priority.

Heavenly Father, stir my heart in the direction of daily, uncompromised obedience to Your will. Shift my attention outward so that I reach out and help the lost who are near me. I pray this in Jesus' name, amen.

Fully Surrendered

Fully surrendered—Lord, I would be,
Fully surrendered, dear Lord, to Thee.
All on the altar laid,
Surrender fully made,
Thou hast my ransom paid;
I yield to Thee.

Fully surrendered—life, time, and all,
All Thou hast given me held at Thy call.
Speak but the word to me,
Gladly I'll follow Thee,
Now and eternally
Obey my Lord.

Fully surrendered—silver and gold,
His, who hath given me riches untold.
All, all belong to Thee,
For Thou didst purchase me,
Thine evermore to be,
Jesus, my Lord.

Fully surrendered—Lord I am Thine;
Fully surrendered, Savior divine!
Live Thou Thy life in me;
All fullness dwells in Thee;
Not I, but Christ in me,
Christ all in all.

Alfred C. Snead

3

Cultivating a Life of Obedience

Ye adulterers and adulteresses, know ye not that the friend-ship of the world is enmity with God? whosoever therefore will be a friend of the world is the enemy of God.

James 4:4

It appears to me that there's been a lack of kind generos-ity among many in churches today. We must keep in mind, however, that if we as followers of the Lord are to cultivate a life of obedience, we have been called by Him to love and to serve the simplest, poorest people and never to look down on them. We must remember the way in which Jesus gathered around himself the poor and destitute; He did not turn such people away but treated them with dignity.

A woman in my church once came to me and said, "Pastor, I think I'm going to attend another church." When I asked her why, she responded, "It's not that there's anything wrong with the preaching or the fellowship. But I've noticed that people who aren't dressed well don't feel comfortable coming here. There are a lot of poor kids whose mothers can't dress them up, and when they come to Sunday school, they're dressed in pretty shoddy condition. I'm afraid they won't feel welcome here. As I visit people in the neighborhood, I hesitate to invite those ones who don't have nice clothes."

I went to the congregation to talk about this woman's concern. If true, it would be a terrible charge against our church. We should never cause those who do not have much money to feel unwelcome, as if they don't belong. I did everything I could to rectify that situation, for all people are Christian brethren or potential Christian brethren. That's all that ought to matter.

I pray there will never be a moment when the poor among us feel unwelcome. The poorest of the poor, those who lack life's basic necessities, should always be made to feel at home in the Christian Church. I pray we will not ignore such people but instead show "the least of these" acceptance, kindness, and great care (see Matthew 25:40). I think of the hymn by Philip Doddridge:

Do Not I Love Thee, O My Lord?

Do not I love Thee, O my Lord?
Behold my heart and see;
And turn each cursed idol out,
That dares to rival Thee.

Hast Thou a lamb in all Thy flock
I would disdain to feed?
Hast Thou a foe, before whose face
I fear Thy cause to plead?

Another attribute of obedience has to do with our relationship to the world. Too often our everyday living reflects an underlying worldliness—that is, the world tends to influence our conduct and hinder our obedience. In James 4:4 we read, "Ye adulterers and adulteresses, know ye not that the friendship of the world is enmity with God? whosoever therefore will be a friend of the world is the enemy of God."

We can be orthodox in our doctrine, emphasize the Lord as being all in all, and still maintain an attitude toward the world that is fundamentally unchristian. We must be wary of worldliness taking root in our churches. I believe we ought to watch for this, pray fervently about it, preach against it, and do what we can to resist it.

There is also the danger of lukewarmness, which can negatively affect our obedience. However, the intensity of our spiritual desire will surely break down any such hindrances and defeat every foe, creating a vacuum into which the Holy Spirit can rush in. Our spiritual desire will coincide with self-sacrifice and obedience and will drive us toward a greater intimacy with the Lord Jesus.

Perhaps we first need to break up our fallow ground. But what is fallow ground? It is ground that was once fruitful and is good ground still, but it hasn't been plowed or used for several years, and it's been rain-hardened and sun-beaten.

Now it's just lying there, nothing grows on it, just a few weeds and briars, and yet it remains good ground. It's not producing because no seeds have been planted in it, and it's not been plowed in a long time. It takes a lot of plowing to ready a field for planting.

In Psalm 129:3, David said, "The plowers plowed upon my back: they made long their furrows." He felt as though he was lying on his stomach and his enemies had a plow, plowing up and down his back—a very unpleasant experience. His enemies did this to David, but the Holy Spirit teaches us that we are to do it to ourselves. We are to break up the fallow ground of our hearts and seek the Lord. And the seed of the Lord, when it falls, will produce great fruit.

The harvest season lies before us. Godliness and prayer, self-sacrifice and hard work—these are never out of season in the kingdom of God. Lost souls should grieve us, fill us with prayer and burden us until our hearts are plowed up. Reaching the lost with the gospel of Christ should motivate all that we do. In the end, what matters most is our faithfulness to what God has called us to. So let's break up our fallow ground and continue to follow the Lord in obedience.

Let us learn from the people of Israel, who at one point had turned their backs on their obedience to God. News came to a faithful priest named Ezra that the people were intermarrying and doing all sorts of things they shouldn't be doing, such as working on the Sabbath day and not attending the Temple. When Ezra heard about this, he dropped to his knees before God in sackcloth and ashes, plucked his beard, and pulled his hair.

He didn't pull anyone else's hair but his own, and he didn't pull the hair of Israel (see Ezra 10). And so we must first work on ourselves before God, making sure we are where we should be in our hearts, and if necessary repent of our sin and complacency and ask God to set things right again.

I pray we may receive a new baptism of His power, His light, and His presence in our lives.

Heavenly Father, it's my desire to move forward in my Christian experience every day. Help me to cultivate my Christian life by obeying You in every aspect that's important to You. I pray this in Jesus' name, amen.

Stand Up, Stand Up for Jesus

Stand up, stand up for Jesus
ye soldiers of the cross;
lift high his royal banner,
it must not suffer loss.
From vict'ry unto vict'ry
his army he shall lead
till ev'ry foe is vanquished
and Christ is Lord indeed.

Stand up, stand up for Jesus,
the trumpet call obey;
forth to the mighty conflict
in this his glorious day.
Ye that are men now serve him
against unnumbered foes;
let courage rise with danger
and strength to strength oppose.

Stand up, stand up for Jesus,
stand in his strength alone;
the arm of flesh will fail you,
ye dare not trust your own.
Put on the gospel armor,
each piece put on with prayer;
where duty calls or danger,
be never wanting there.

Stand up, stand up for Jesus,
the strife will not be long;
this day the noise of battle,
the next, the victor's song.
To him that overcometh
a crown of life shall be;
he with the King of glory
shall reign eternally.

George Duffield

4

Compromising Our Obedience

Therefore let all the house of Israel know assuredly,
that God hath made the same Jesus, whom ye have
crucified, both Lord and Christ.

Acts 2:36

One of the most critical aspects of our obedience is knowing who Jesus Christ really is. Not what the world describes Him to be but what the Word of God reveals Him to be. Our obedience becomes compromised when we don't understand Jesus and know Him for who He is according to the Scriptures.

Here is something I consider to be bad teaching: first, we are saved by accepting Christ as our Savior; second, we are sanctified by accepting Christ as our Lord. We may do the first without doing the second. I have been taught this, and I've found it is woven into a lot of Christian literature.

Many who preach to young people and exhort them to consecrate themselves to God, to fully surrender and be filled with the Holy Spirit, begin by saying, "You are saved now, and that's good. You were saved by taking Jesus Christ as your Savior; you will be filled with His Spirit when you take Him as your Lord."

The implication is that they can take Him as their Savior without taking Him as their Lord. But this is far from being the case, as it's founded on the flawed doctrine that Christ may sustain a divided relationship with us, that our Lord Jesus Christ can be our Savior without being our Lord, and that we can be saved without obeying the sovereign Lord.

Now, what the Bible says about this is that "God hath made the same Jesus, whom ye have crucified, both Lord and Christ" (Acts 2:36). Therefore, "Jesus" means *Savior*, "Lord" means *sovereign*, and "Christ" means *anointed one*. Simply put, Jesus is Savior, Lord, and Christ; and He never divides His offices.

Romans 10:8–9 states, "But what saith it? The word is nigh thee, even in thy mouth, and in thy heart: that is, the word of faith, which we preach; That if thou shalt confess with thy mouth the Lord Jesus, and shalt believe in thine heart that God hath raised him from the dead, thou shalt be saved."

You'll notice the apostle Paul didn't say "thou shalt confess with thy mouth the Savior." No, he said, "thou shalt confess with thy mouth the Lord Jesus."

He goes on to say, "For with the heart man believeth unto righteousness; and with the mouth confession is made unto salvation. For the scripture saith, Whosoever believeth on him shall not be ashamed. For there is no difference between the Jew and the Greek: for the same Lord over all is rich unto all that call upon him. For whosoever shall call upon the name of the Lord shall be saved" (Romans 10:10–13).

This passage refers to Jesus as "Lord" three times in telling us how we might be saved. The Scripture clearly teaches that faith in the Lord Jesus and confession of that faith to the world brings salvation to us. So the Bible doesn't adopt the position that the different offices of Jesus Christ can be divided in any way, as if a person could receive Him today as Savior and then ten years from now get around to accepting Him as their Lord.

In 1 Peter 1:1–2, we read, "Peter, an apostle of Jesus Christ . . . elect according to the foreknowledge of God the Father, through sanctification of the Spirit, unto obedience and sprinkling of the blood of Jesus Christ: Grace unto you, and peace, be multiplied." Salvation apart from obedience, then, is unheard of in the Scriptures.

Still, some continue to assert the opposite, saying, "Come to Him. You don't have to obey—you don't have to change anything, do anything, give up anything, surrender anything, give back anything. Just come to Him and believe in Him as your Savior." And so they come and believe. Later, they attend a deeper-life conference, where somebody tells them, "You who have received Jesus as Savior, how would you like to take him as your Lord now?" How utterly misguided this is. It leads people to believe in a divided Christ when of course no one can receive half of Christ.

Furthermore, the Bible never tells us that we're to believe in an office or a work, but we're to believe in the Lord who did that work and holds those offices. When a person places their faith and trust in Jesus Christ, they must believe in the *whole* Lord Jesus Christ without reservation.

Yet some Christians think of Jesus as a kind of divine nurse. They go to Him when sin has made them sick and plead, "Lord, if you may, please help me," and He blessedly does it, after which they say thank you and go their way. But nowhere in the Scriptures can such a concept be found. Again, our obedience rests on who we believe Jesus Christ is.

Rather, the Bible speaks of Jesus as both Savior and Lord. And as the Lord, he saves us because He holds all the offices of Savior and Christ, as well as "high priest" of wisdom, righteousness, sanctification, and redemption (see Hebrews 2:17 and 4:14). He's all of these, embodied in Him as Christ the Lord, the authority of our obedience.

Our obedience demands that we receive all of Christ. We must accept either all of Him or reject Him altogether. Either He's Lord of all or He's not Lord at all. We often overlook the fact that we all come to Him as sinners, rebels against the Most High God. We're sons of disobedience. Sin is the breaking of the just laws of God, and we're in rebellion. And while we are sinners, we're fugitives from His divine justice.

The root of sin, then, is our rebellion against God's laws. It says, "I belong to myself. I owe allegiance to nobody unless I choose to give it." That's the essence of sin. But salvation reverses this and restores the relationship between the sinner and God. The first thing the returning sinner does is to pray, "Father, I have sinned against heaven, and before thee, and am no more worthy to be called thy son: make me as one of thy hired servants" (Luke 15:18–19).

Through repentance we reverse this situation and meekly submit to God's Word and will. Then we believe and are saved. The believer's happiness and security rests in their obedience to God.

Psalm 103:20 says, "Bless the LORD, ye his angels, that excel in strength, that do his commandments, hearkening unto the voice of his word." The very angels in heaven find their complete freedom and happiness in obeying the commandments of God. Instead of seeing it as tyranny, they find it a delight.

I've been studying the first chapter of Ezekiel. It's a mystery, and I confess I don't fully understand it. There are creatures with four faces, four wings, and odd-looking beings doing odd things. They have wheels, with more wheels at the center of those wheels. There is fire coming out of the north, winged creatures doing various things, and all are strange and beautiful as they have the time of their lives.

But the one thing I do understand is that they are utterly delighted by the presence of God and that they could serve God. Heaven is a place of total surrender to the whole will of God, and it's heaven because it is such a place.

Everything else that can be said about hell may be true, but this one thing is its essence: hell is the world of disobedience, the world of the rebel. Hell is the Alcatraz for the unreconstructed rebels who would not surrender to the will of God, whereas heaven is heaven because it is the realm of obedient children—the children of the Most High God.

Hell is hell not just because of worms and fire (see Mark 9:48), although I believe both are there because Jesus said they were. You might endure worms and fire, but for a moral creature to know that he's where he is because he's a rebel is the true punishment. He has no self-respect left, no hope left, no nobility left, nothing. He's being held in the world of the disobedient.

Each person must decide which world he's going to inhabit. He's got to decide now while he's still alive. So let us not go sprightly and cheerfully to the Lord Jesus and say, "I'm coming for some help, and I understand you're the Savior. I'm going to believe in you and be saved," and then turn away and say, "I'll think about the other matter later."

I warn you, you'll get no help, for the Lord will not save those whom He cannot command. He will not divide His offices. You cannot believe in half a Christ. We must take Him for what and who He is, the anointed Savior and Lord, the King of kings and Lord of lords, who saves us with the understanding that He will also guide our lives going forward by His Spirit.

Under Finney and Wesley and such men as this, people would only dare to call themselves a Christian if they had surrendered their whole being to God, taken Jesus Christ as Lord as well as Savior, repented and brought themselves under obedience to the will of the Lord. Only then could one say with confidence, "I'm saved."

But today some claim they're saved without obedience. Then later on, we talk about the deeper life and say, "Now let's consider Jesus' lordship." Don't you think you owe Him your obedience right away? You owe Him obedience from the second you came to Him for salvation.

If we do not submit and give Him our obedience, I have a reason to wonder if we're really converted. I see people do things and watch them operate, and I'm made to question whether they're converted or not or ever were. Perhaps they imagine the Lord as the chief of staff at a hospital, there to fix up poor sinners who get themselves in trouble. Such thinking only leads to self-deception.

Let us not go blindly on our way, believing we are saved when perhaps we're not. You may have believed imperfectly in a divided Savior, which of course is no Savior at all. Let us instead gaze at Him who wears the crowns, the Lord of all lords and King of all kings forever, the One who has a perfect moral right to full obedience from all of His saved people.

Heavenly Father, I praise Thee for the complete salvation You have provided through Your Son, the Lord Jesus Christ, for all who sincerely follow and obey Him. May my heart always be in full compliance to Your Word. In Jesus' name I pray, amen.

I Choose Thee, Blessed Will of God

I choose Thee, blessed will of God!
In Thee alone, my heart can rest,
The current of Thy love, I know
Can only bear me to Thy breast.

I choose Thee, blessed will of God!
In Thee alone, my heart can rest.

I choose Thee, blessed will of God!
No longer shall this will of mine
In selfish blindness to Thy love,
Its hateful choice and strength combine.

I choose Thee, blessed will of God!
The sweetest thing my heart hath known
A chariot my God hath sent
To bear me upward to His throne.

I choose Thee, blessed will of God!
For in the circling of Thine arms,
The gladdest Spring of Joy I find;
Outside Thee fears and strange alarms.

May A. Stephens

5

As Obedient Children

"As obedient children, not fashioning yourselves according to the former lusts in your ignorance. . . ."

1 Peter 1:14

With those words "As obedient children," we enter into, rather unceremoniously, a long apostolic exhortation for believers to take action. Peter mentions such things as hope, pursuing holiness, and loving one another.

Take a moment to think about the phrase *as obedient children.* Notice how there is no verb associated with this phrase; he doesn't say *"be* obedient." He is not exhorting us here to be obedient. Instead, he says, "As obedient children, do so and so."

I point this out to show that Peter is assuming obedience because they are believers. When Peter wrote to the brethren who were elect according to the foreknowledge of God, given the fact that they were indeed brethren, he assumed that they were elect. And since they were saved unto obedience, he trusted they would then be obedient children.

He did not say, "Now be obedient," although this could very well be stated elsewhere in Scripture. What I'm saying is that Peter did not say this here. Rather, he said, "Assuming you are believers, I therefore gather that you are also obedient."

Obedience, which is taught throughout the Bible, is one of the most demanding requirements of the Christian life. For apart from obedience, there can be no salvation. Salvation without obedience is a self-contradictory impossibility because, as I said earlier, the essence of sin is rebellion against God and His divine authority.

"And the LORD God commanded the man, saying, Of every tree of the garden thou mayest freely eat: But of the tree of the knowledge of good and evil, thou shalt not eat of it: for in the day that thou eatest thereof thou shalt surely die" (Genesis 2:16–17). Adam and Eve, despite the strong prohibition given to them here, stretched forth their hands regardless and tasted of the fruit.

They disobeyed and rebelled, and in their rebellion they brought sin upon themselves, as sin and rebellion are synonymous in God's eyes. It says in Romans 5:12, "Wherefore, as by one man sin entered into the world, and death by sin; and so death passed upon all men, for that all have sinned." One man's disobedience brought about the downfall of the world.

In 1 John 3:4, we read, "Whosoever committeth sin transgresseth also the law: for sin is the transgression of the law." In plain English, sin is disobedience to the law of God. And Ephesians 2:2 says, "Wherein in time past ye walked according to the course of this world, according to the prince of the power of the air, the spirit that now worketh in the children of disobedience. . . ."

The word *children* here isn't about physical age; it is an idiomatic expression. It's similar to when we sing about the Americans being the sons and daughters of freedom. When we say that the people of the world are children of disobedience, we mean disobedience characterizes them. They breathe disobedience—it colors them, it conditions them, and it molds them. It is an intrinsic part of who and what they are.

The whole question before the human race is, *Who is boss?* This can be broken down into a series of further questions. More specifically, "To whom do I belong? To whom do I owe allegiance? Who has the authority to require obedience of me?"

Those are three important questions, and we Americans, among all the peoples of the world, are some of the hardest people to get to obey anybody because we are the sons and daughters of freedom.

We are the offshoot of a revolt against the Crown. We poured tea into the Boston Harbor, and we made speeches and said we would not sit idly by and wear the chains of the British. Then came the famous words, "Give me liberty or give me death."

This idea is in our blood, and so when anyone demands, "You owe obedience," we Americans bristle immediately. We want it explained to us because we don't take kindly to our having to be obedient to anyone. Likewise, the children of the world have their answer ready to the questions "Who is boss?" and "To whom do I belong?" That answer is simply, "I am boss; I belong to myself."

We make a great deal out of what we call *individualism*. We believe in the right to self-determination. If we are asked, "To whom do I owe allegiance?" our answer is quick and to the point: "I owe allegiance to nobody." And the answer to the question, "Who has authority to require obedience of me?" again is "No one."

This rings of the liberty and freedom of the American attitude and way of life, but it can also act as a snare. For while God has given us the *power* of self-determination, He has not given us the *right* of self-determination.

Free will means that God has given us the power of self-determination. He gave this to Adam and Eve when He said, "That tree with the fruit is right there. You have free will. You can do as you please, roam at will, go to sleep, get up and eat what you please, but with one exception. I forbid you to eat of that tree."

So they had the power of self-determination, but they did not have the right to self-determination. There is an important difference.

If God had not granted us the power of self-determination, then we would be automatons. Machines, not human beings. A machine has no power of self-determination. Though it may have cost a million dollars, it will sit where it is until it rusts out. It'll only move from there if you or somebody else moves it. An airplane in the sky has no power of self-determination. A pilot controls the plane and determines where it will fly to; the plane has no power to determine its own destiny.

If God had made us like robots, automobiles, airplanes, or some other type of machine, then we would not have the power of self-determination. But since He made us moral creatures, created in His own image, He has given us the power of self-determination (see Genesis 1:27).

But again this is not the same as a right. I keep using the word *right* because I often hear it in political speeches or read about it in related literature. But what's truly meant is a *power* and not a right.

We have, then, the power of self-determination because God has given us the power to choose good or evil, but that doesn't mean we have the right to choose evil. For example, no person has any right to lie. We have the power to lie, but not the right. Or we have the power to say, "I can go to the store and steal myself a better coat than the one I have now," just slip out the back door and get away with it. You may have that power, but you do not have the right.

You only have a right to be good; you never have a right to be bad because God is good. You only have a right to be holy; you never have a right to be unholy. If you're unholy, you usurp a right that is not yours. Adam and Eve had no moral right to eat of the tree that God had forbidden them to eat from, but they did so anyway.

Lord Tennyson, in his long poem *In Memoriam A. H. H.*, wrote the lines:

> Thou seemest human and divine,
> The highest, holiest manhood, thou.
> Our wills are ours, we know not how;
> Our wills are ours, to make them thine.

Here, Tennyson acknowledges that we have wills which belong to us, but then he writes "we know not how." It's beyond us, this deep mystery of man's free will. It's all too much for us to comprehend.

47

The only real *right* we have is to make our wills the will of God, or rather to make the will of God our will. That way, we do not violate our will; we purify our will. We do not destroy it; we sanctify it by submitting our power of self-determination in obedience and worship to our Creator.

Finally, we don't have the right of self-determination because we are what we are, and God is who and what He is. God is sovereign; we are His creatures. He's the Creator and therefore He has a right to command, and we have an obligation to obey Him. Yet it's a happy obligation.

Heavenly Father, it's my privilege to bow before Thee in humble obedience to Thy will. Help me to love Thee more every day, to align my life with Thy will each morning I get up. May my life and my obedience bring You pleasure. In Jesus' name I pray, amen.

I'll Live for Him

My life, my love I give to Thee,
Thou Lamb of God who died for me;
O may I ever faithful be,
My Savior and my God!

I'll live for him who died for me,
How happy then my life shall be!
I'll live for him who died for me,
My Savior and my God!

I now believe thou dost receive,
For Thou hast died that I might live;
And now henceforth I'll trust in Thee,
My Savior and my God!

O Thou who died on Calvary,
To save my soul and make me free;
I'll consecrate my life to Thee,
My Savior and my God!

R. E. Hudson

6

The Environment
for Our Obedience

Then they that gladly received his word were baptized: and the same day there were added unto them about three thousand souls. And they continued steadfastly in the apostles' doctrine and fellowship, and in breaking of bread, and in prayers. And fear came upon every soul: and many wonders and signs were done by the apostles. And all that believed were together, and had all things common; and sold their possessions and goods, and parted them to all men, as every man had need. And they, continuing daily with one accord in the temple, and breaking bread from house to house, did eat their meat with gladness and singleness of heart, praising God, and having favour with all the people. And the Lord added to the church daily such as should be saved.

Acts 2:41–47

For something to stay healthy, it needs to be in a healthy environment. If the vegetables in your garden are to grow and thrive, they must be in an environment that cultivates growth.

This principle also applies to our spiritual lives. Our attitude of obedience has to be placed in a healthy environment that enables it to grow according to the pleasure of God himself. This chapter focuses on verse 42: "And they continued steadfastly in the apostles' doctrine and fellowship, and in breaking of bread, and in prayers."

The Church here is called to be in fellowship. Let us now consider the New Testament definition of the word *fellowship*, wherein it means "a sharing together." But even more than that, fellowship is to include an intimate sharing together, a communion of the heart and the mind.

This communion of hearts and minds among Christians is taught in the Scriptures. Ephesians 3:15 says, "Of whom the whole family in heaven and earth is named." Later, in Ephesians 4:3–4, we read, "Endeavouring to keep the unity of the Spirit in the bond of peace. There is one body, and one Spirit, even as ye are called in one hope of your calling. . . ."

Before there can be communion, there must be *union*. And this union of believers can be seen throughout the Scriptures and is repeated in our Christian creeds. I know some shy away from creeds, and some even say they don't believe in them. I smile when I hear others say things like, "I don't like creeds; I stay with the Bible," because a creed is just a system of Christian beliefs. Every time you stand to testify, beginning with "I believe," you are stating your creed even if you don't think it's your creed.

Our Christian creeds consist of sound biblical truth, carefully assembled by some of the holiest and most learned men

in the Church. And one of the assertions in the Apostles'
Creed states, "I believe in the communion of saints."

I don't believe in communication with dead saints; I believe in the *communion* of all the saints in heaven and on
earth. They are still in our communion, and we are in theirs.
We're not in communication, which means you cannot be
put into some sort of trance and communicate with someone
who has died. But if that person was a Christian, you can
still be in full fellowship and communion with them in all
that they were and stood for and where they are now.

There remains an unbroken spiritual communion. Distance may divide matter, but it does not divide spirit—that
is, we as believers can yet be one in the Spirit with someone
who has died and gone to heaven to be with the Lord. All
those in the Christian Church are one in the Spirit, around
the world and in heaven.

The Church's One Foundation

Yet she on earth hath union
With God the Three in One,
And mystic sweet communion
With those whose rest is won:
O happy ones and holy!
Lord, give us grace that we,
Like them, the meek and lowly,
In love may dwell with Thee.

Samuel J. Stone

Protestants, and particularly evangelicals, in eagerness to
be rid of formality and ritual, have thrown out a great many
gold nuggets along with a few things that should have been

thrown out. It's mighty nice to remember that we believe in the communion of saints and that the saints of God enjoy union now with all of God's children. That is true ecumenical Christianity.

Some people believe that the Bible talks about the union of all Christians into one great super-church. This is not biblical, as we don't need to unite the Church. The true Church is already united in a sweet communion that has never been separated.

This unity can be divided into six separate unities. These six unities describe the healthy environment in which we should share in fellowship as the Church of Jesus Christ.

The first one is the *fellowship of truth*, and the fellowship of God's people revolves around God's truth, which is centered in the sacred revelation of the Scriptures. The holy Book of God is a gold mine that has never been fully explored and contains all the riches that we need in heaven and earth, for God's Word is that center around which all our fellowship moves.

If it is written in the Bible, that is enough. We desire nothing beyond the Scriptures and want nothing less than what the Scriptures offer. And we reject anything and everything contrary to the Scriptures.

Second, we not only have the fellowship of truth but we have the *fellowship of life*. The true Church is a fellowship of life. Nobody is in the Church except for those who have been baptized into the Church and the life of God in the Holy Spirit. Life comes from God, and when life comes, then we are baptized into one body.

Each individual church around the world as well as the Church as a whole are more than organizations; they are organisms of life. There is a life that makes the Church a real organism. We have this fellowship; we share together the life of Jesus Christ by the Holy Spirit—the marvelous life that couldn't stay in the grave but came forth in glory and splendor on the third day.

Third, we have the *fellowship of a presence*. We have been taught in the Scriptures that Jesus is in the midst of us. Matthew 18:20 says, "For where two or three are gathered together in my name, there am I in the midst of them."

We assemble together in the house or habitation of God through the Holy Spirit. We don't meet each Sunday in the name of a minister on the platform; we meet in the name of another, Jesus Christ, who is ever present and unseen.

And if we are sensitive enough to the Holy Spirit, we can feel His presence among us. We know He's there with us at that moment because He's promised in His Word that He will never leave us nor forsake us (see Deuteronomy 31:6 and Hebrews 13:5). We can rest assured, then, of His divine communion.

For we believe these Scriptures to be true, that we can come to know His glorious presence in our lives—that is, in conscious experience. Placing all of our trust in His Word, we are confident that we have the fellowship of His presence not only in the house of God but at home or at work or wherever we find ourselves. He promises to be with us no matter the circumstance or geography.

This is especially true, however, when a group of Christians meet together. The Lord is in His holy Temple; God is among us and is with us. Together we share the presence and beauty of the unseen Lord, the Son of the Living God, Jesus Christ, as well as the Holy Spirit, the Comforter.

So we have this communal worship, and yet worshiping together as a community is only as perfect as the private worship is back home. If you take a thousand people who do not pray during the week and bring them together and have them attempt a fellowship of worship, they may approximate it, but they won't have much success. You are not more holy because you're in church; you're only as holy as you were when you came to church.

I think of the hymn by Isaac Watts:

> **Blessing God for His Goodness**
> Bless, O my soul, the living God,
> Call home thy thoughts that rove abroad,
> Let all the pow'rs within me join
> In work and worship so divine,
> In work and worship so divine.

As we meet in the fellowship of worship, our attention and our thoughts should be centered on the Lord Jesus Christ. If we would only concentrate on that wonderful unseen presence, worshiping Him with all of our hearts, the Lord is sure to bless our gathering and in unexpected ways.

Fourth, there is the *fellowship of love*. This is a love felt toward God first of all, followed by a love felt toward those who are lost. This love is something that cannot come from the world. When we gather together in fellowship, there is an atmosphere of love that motivates that fellowship. If there is someone I cannot love, there is nobody I can truly love, and I don't understand the love of God.

Of course, our love begins with Christ himself: His love for us and our love responding back to Him. When we love

Christ, it will be reflected in our love for our brothers and sisters in the Lord. We love them not because of who they are, but because of who Christ is.

As we gather together in the Spirit and in fellowship, we can look out and see those lost souls who are in need of fellowship. And as our love for Christ grows deeper, so too does our love for others.

Fifth is the *fellowship of service.* We meet on the Lord's Day so that we might recharge our batteries to serve. Jesus Christ was anointed of God by the Holy Spirit, and He went about doing good and healing all that the devil had oppressed. He went about doing good after He was anointed, and the anointing enabled Him to do great things. We must also do this, for as Christ came into the world to serve others, so are we as His followers in this world to serve.

What kind of service have we rendered to the Lord? The cup of water given to the thirsty in the Master's name will not go unrewarded. Any money given to care for the poor and hungry, or given to the mission spreading the gospel around the globe, or given to helping children who have been displaced because of political upheavals throughout the world—none of this will go unrewarded by our Lord.

Sixth and last, there's the *fellowship of the new creation.* This fellowship comes from God and is sacred and therefore won't be of much interest to those who are worldly-minded, to the lovers of money and of pleasure.

How wonderful it is to have a fellowship where Christ is, to know that you don't have to search for truth—you have truth. To know that you worship because you have His presence, and you serve not because you might be saved but because you are saved and enjoy the new creation.

I pray that we grow in unity and in grace, that our hearts will remain tuned in to the presence of Jesus Christ, as this is who and what we are seeking. When we receive communion around the table together in a sweet but real way, we take of His body and drink of His blood and share in the faith. All of this nourishes our obedience to the Lord. And without obedience, none of this would be a reality in our lives.

Heavenly Father, I praise Thee for the fellowship where I can enjoy Thy presence and honor Thee through my obedience. Thank Thee for all that You've done and for blessing me and those of my fellowship. In Jesus' name I pray, amen.

Obedience

By Thy blessed word obeying,
Lord, we prove our love sincere;
For we hear Thee gently saying,
"Love will do as well as hear."

Dear Redeemer, we would hallow
All Thy word so firm and true;
In Thy footsteps meekly follow,
Thy commands we love to do.

Feigned hearts Thy name professing,
Thy commandments cast aside;
But we feel Thy great salvation,
And in all Thy truth abide.

Every word Thy mouth hath spoken
Is essential to our life;
All Thy mandates love betoken,
To oppose them is but strife.

In Thy wisdom, Lord, confiding,
We will follow in Thy way;
With Thy love in us abiding,
'Tis delightful to obey.

Each commandment Thou hast given
Is a waymark on the road;
Leading up from earth to heaven,
To the blessed throne of God.

Daniel S. Warner

7

The God Who Deserves Our Obedience

Thine, O LORD, is the greatness, and the power, and the glory, and the victory, and the majesty: for all that is in the heaven and in the earth is thine; thine is the kingdom, O LORD, and thou art exalted as head above all.

1 Chronicles 29:11

Canst thou by searching find out God? canst thou find out the Almighty unto perfection? It is as high as heaven; what canst thou do? deeper than hell; what canst thou know?

Job 11:7–8

Lo, these are parts of his ways: but how little a portion is heard of him? but the thunder of his power who can understand?

Job 26:14

Which in his times he shall shew, who is the blessed and only Potentate, the King of kings, and Lord of lords; Who only hath immortality, dwelling in the light which no man can approach unto; whom no man hath seen, nor can see: to whom be honour and power everlasting. Amen.

1 Timothy 6:15–16

Some theologians have a way of hiding the truth behind big words. For example, *divine transcendence* simply means that God is above you. And *omnipresence* means He is everywhere. He's just as close to you as your breath; He's closer to you than your very soul. Your little thoughts are heard by Him just as loud as your loudest shouts because God is as near to you as your blood, your nerves, your musings, and your spirit.

And yet God is so high up that He cannot be conceived by human beings. What I mean by "high up" or "far above" has nothing to do with distance. God doesn't care anything about distance. No, He's high up in the sense that He has an extraordinary existence that's infinitely beyond our own.

When we think about God, we must not imagine Him perched away somewhere on a star or in some far-distant imperium, as the ancient Greeks did. We must imagine Him as extraordinary and supernatural, but also as present. God can take the entire universe and place it in the palm of His hand.

Also, God is above us in the sense that God's life is infinitely above ours. It's a mistake to think of God as simply occupying the peak in an ascending scale of life. We begin with a cell and think our way up to the fish, then think our way up a little further to the bird, then think our way up to the beast.

Thus we have an ascending scale of life. From there we think our way up to man, then on up to angels, archangels, the cherubim and the seraphim. And then at the very top of that ascending scale stands God.

No, that is incorrect or inaccurate.

Would you be shocked if I said that God is just as far above an archangel as He is above a caterpillar? You see, the gap that separates the archangel from the caterpillar is finite. The archangel was certainly given a greater life and is far higher than the caterpillar, but they are alike in that they are creatures. There was a time when they didn't exist, and then they did. The archangel with his broad wings and the tiny caterpillar inching its way along are both creatures of God.

But God is *not* a creature, and He doesn't belong in the creature category at all. We must think of God as separate from, high above, other than, and beyond all other creatures in the cosmos. He is God; there is nothing and no one like Him. That which is God, the substance of the Creator, has no parallel in all the universe.

The substance of God is wholly unique in that He can never pass away and cease to be God. And any other thing, person, or entity that is not God can ever become God. Jesus was God and man united, but there will never be such a thing as man becoming God, just as there will never be such a thing as God becoming a creature.

The everlasting God is beyond all speech and all thought: God the Father, the Son, and the Holy Spirit, the "Alpha and Omega, the beginning and the ending . . . which is, and which was, and which is to come, the Almighty" (Revelation 1:8). Heaven and earth are full of the majesty of God's glory.

The cherubim and seraphim, together with the angels, continually cry, "Holy, holy, holy, Lord God Almighty." The prophets, the saints, and the martyrs praise Him with glad hearts, as do the apostles and the Church throughout all the world. He is a good God, the God we're called to serve.

Yet all of this is only a small portion of God, His ways and His character. They are what we would call the rational element, the parts you can get ahold of in your head.

Many people would like to pull God down and make Him the same size they are. They want to chum up with Him and make Him a pal so that they can have a God their size. Or maybe they'd have Him be a little bigger, so he'd help them out when they're in trouble, but not too big that they would be afraid of Him.

More often than not, that's the kind of God being dished out these days in Christian churches throughout the country. The God of the average church is too small. He is not the God of heaven and creation, and not the God of the Bible, but a homemade God pulled down to our human level. He's a religious version of Santa Claus.

And we want to keep on His good side so that when the time comes, He will make us rich, help us to become successful in business, help us win a game or a prize, and bless us with a rewarding life. We think of Him being around to keep the stars in place and the rivers flowing, like a divine janitor looking after things, there to step in and fix whatever needs fixing.

But I wouldn't bend the knee to that kind of God. No, that kind does not deserve my obedience. The God who can get me on my knees must be infinitely higher than I am. He has to be so mighty that He can take the world in His hands and shake it. He has to be infinitely more powerful than the devil and infinitely greater than any earthly king.

I don't bow to people easily. I don't like the idea of class; this is not the way to be a Christian. God made us all, and the humblest little child is just as valuable to God as a stuffed shirt with lots of money who can write big checks and drive expensive cars. Let's remember that people are not to be classified.

But God is different. When it comes to Almighty God, instantly we're on our knees. Instantly we bow because He's infinitely higher than all. How shall we forlorn mortals dare to sing to this great God?

Lord Jesus Christ, We Seek Thy Face

Lord Jesus Christ, we seek Thy face;
Within the veil we bow the knee;
O let Thy glory fill the place!
And bless us while we wait on Thee.

Alexander Stewart

Jesus Christ is God walking among men and women, receiving children into His arms. When they nailed Him to the cross, He had created the nails they used to put Him there. He had caused the tree to grow from which they made a cross to hang Him on. He died in shame for our sins on that very tree.

He is the Lord God, the Almighty, the eternal One without end. So when we say "accept Jesus as Lord," we're not doing Jesus any favors. Some preachers make it sound as though you'll be doing Jesus a great favor to come to Him.

65

You don't do Jesus any favors when you give your heart to Him, and He doesn't lose anything if you refuse to give your heart to Him. Withhold your love, and He's lost nothing. Give your love and He gains nothing. He already has the world without end.

We're not doing Jesus any favors by testifying, witnessing, or giving our hearts to Him. But He's doing us an infinite favor in stooping to receive us to His bosom. The Almighty, transcendent God stooped to be man; He stooped to die and yet rose again.

In the Old Testament, four letters, Y-H-W-H, were used when referring to God. The people didn't try to pronounce it as a word, and so over time people have come to refer to God using transliterated words such as *Jehovah* or *Yahweh*. These four letters were called the Tetragrammaton, or the incommunicable name. Y-H-W-H occurs many times in the Bible. But those reverent, Old Testament Jews didn't want every Tom, Dick, and Harry pronouncing that awesome name, so it has since been translated as "Lord."

With God there should be a sense of dread. Theologians and philosophers have referred to the transcendent God as the *mysterium tremendum*, a Latin phrase that means "mystery that repels." This describes a mystery that is both awe-inspiring and overwhelming, a mystery before which humanity trembles and is fascinated by simultaneously. It was before this *mysterium tremendum* that Jacob became afraid, saying, "How dreadful is this place! this is none other but the house of God, and this is the gate of heaven" (Genesis 28:17).

Simon Peter, astonished by the catch of fish they had taken at Jesus' command to "put out into the deep and let down your nets," and sensing the *mysterium tremendum*, "fell down at Jesus' knees, saying, 'Depart from me; for I am a sinful man, O Lord'" (Luke 5:8).

Abraham as well went to pieces before God and said, "Behold now, I have taken upon me to speak unto the LORD, which am but dust and ashes" (Genesis 18:27).

Job, too, when before God, became like a man stricken and was rendered speechless. "Behold, I am vile; what shall I answer thee? I will lay mine hand upon my mouth" (Job 40:4). Job was a great orator; he could simply open his mouth and the words would flow out like water from a spigot. But when God revealed himself, Job laid his hand on his mouth and stammered, "O God, excuse me, I can't talk."

Do you know why some people are not getting anywhere in their spiritual lives? It's because they've never met that kind of God. Their little God was tailor-made for them, spun out in evangelistic stories like cheap fiction. They have been fed sentimental goofiness to the point where they can no longer recognize the true, awesome nature of God before whom we are all utterly ignorant.

We'll realize just how little we know when one day we are accepted into the awesome presence of the Most High God—the God who knows all that can be known in one easy, effortless act, and He knows it all instantly. None of us knows very much really, and the man who thinks he knows the most is the man who, according to the apostle Paul, knows the least.

If we would simply admit to how profoundly ignorant we truly are before God, we might begin to get somewhere in our walk with Him. Time spent in worship and obedience to God would then become a priority in our daily lives.

O God, I know Thee, and yet there is so much of Thee I do not know or understand. As I yield entirely to the revelation of who You are, Lord Jesus, I obediently search and long for more of Thee. In Your holy name I pray, amen.

Be Thou My Vision

Be thou my vision, O Lord of my heart;
Naught be all else to me save that thou art.
Thou my best thought by day and by night;
Waking or sleeping, thy presence my light.

Be thou my wisdom, and thou my true Word;
I ever with thee and thou with me, Lord.
Thou my great Father, I thy dear child;
Thou in me dwelling, with thee reconciled.

Be thou my breastplate, my sword for the fight;
Be thou my dignity, thou my delight.
Thou my soul's shelter, thou my high tow'r;
Raise thou me Heav'nward, O Pow'r of my pow'r.

Riches I heed not, nor vain, empty praise;
Thou mine inheritance, now and always.
Thou and thou only, first in my heart,
High King of Heaven, my treasure thou art.

High King of Heaven, my victory won,
May I reach Heaven's joys, O bright Heav'ns Sun!
Heart of my heart, whatever befall,
Still be my vision, O Ruler of all.

Eleanor H. Hull

8

Discouragement Cured through Obedience

Have not I commanded thee? Be strong and of a good courage; be not afraid, neither be thou dismayed: for the LORD thy God is with thee whithersoever thou goest.

Joshua 1:9

Behold, the LORD thy God hath set the land before thee: go up and possess it, as the LORD God of thy fathers hath said unto thee; fear not, neither be discouraged.

Deuteronomy 1:21

One of the most fearsome enemies of the Christian is discouragement. This is a powerful enemy not because it's the greatest, but because it's the greatest nuisance. Discouragement holds immense value in the eyes of the devil, probably because it often works when other temptations fail to work.

71

To begin with, it is important to consider this enemy of the soul as a mood and a climate. What are its causes? More important, what are the cures for discouragement?

Discouragement is indeed a mood, which is to say there's an internal climate at work, a ruling emotion. Discouraged persons are not cowards, not in the least, but they have temporarily lost their courage. This experience can be very painful and distressing for those who suffer from it.

And yet for the one battling discouragement, what they are feeling goes beyond emotion; it becomes a position. Unfortunately, it can go even beyond that, becoming an outlook or attitude. There are people who have been discouraged for years. They have a discouraged look on their faces, and the tone of their voice is one of discouragement. And a great many of them are too discouraged to do anything about their situation.

We find discouragement in lots of places, though it should not be present in the Church. With this combination of emotion, disposition, and outlook arises a climate in which nothing much can grow. If you travel to certain parts of the world, you will find bananas, oranges, and avocados. But you won't find such fruits in Canada because the climate there isn't favorable to their success.

Similarly, certain things won't grow in a discouraged heart, and not only that, but the heart itself won't grow. Where there is discouragement, joy cannot grow as well. The Lord's people ought to be joyful, but joy won't grow in a cold, gloomy, damp climate. Neither will power grow there.

There can be no effective activity where discouragement is concerned. There are some churches where this is the prevailing mood among the people. They come to church discouraged, worship and sing as best they can, listen to the sermon, then go home discouraged. While our activity is meant to be effective and joyful, full of spiritual power, the discouraged mood does not favor joy, power, and effective activity. Rather, it favors noxious plants.

Fear is one such plant. In fact, that's what the word *discouragement* means. As courage means not being afraid, discouragement then speaks of the opposite. This fear can easily slip into self-pity or self-engrossment. Discouraged persons tend to turn inward, giving all their attention to themselves, to their own thoughts, feelings, and needs.

A sense of defeatism settles over the discouraged heart as if to suffocate the person, and this is something that can occur in all people no matter their age or gender, no matter their background or education. It is universal. It's like the common cold—everybody's likely to get it at some point.

There are understandable causes for discouragement. In the Bible, there was a man named Elijah who lacked the support of others. If you have the support of others, you're not so likely to become discouraged. But Elijah didn't have any such support.

Maybe you feel as though you don't get one ounce of help at home. Some people come from a Christian home, where their family members are sympathetic and caring, while others don't have that support.

Another cause of Elijah's discouragement was his failure in meeting his goals. When we fail we are tempted to plunge into despair because our ideal was not realized. Perhaps our ideal was too high to begin with. I doubt you have ever heard of a discouraged cow. That's because a cow is content with being a cow, and that is why it'll stay a cow.

Unlike animals, we human beings have high ideals for ourselves, and so we can become deeply disappointed when those ideals don't come to pass, when we don't become who we had hoped to be.

Elijah's error was in his thinking he stood alone when in fact there were thousands of others just like him. When he became discouraged and went into a tailspin, he asked God to grant him his wish for death: "But he himself went a day's journey into the wilderness, and came and sat down under a juniper tree: and he requested for himself that he might die; and said, It is enough; now, O LORD, take away my life; for I am not better than my fathers" (1 Kings 19:4).

It is important to remember that many people are just as discouraged as you are, if not more so. As Christians, given our spiritual state and condition, we know we are secure in Him and are therefore so much better off than those poor ones who remain lost. We must continue to be thankful to God for His saving us, for His presence in our lives. And we must remember that He has the power to lift us out of our discouragement.

The apostle Paul testified, "Notwithstanding the Lord stood with me, and strengthened me; that by me the preaching might be fully known, and that all the Gentiles might hear: and I was delivered out of the mouth of the lion" (2 Timothy 4:17). Amid his discouragement, Paul recognized the Lord and gave Him the glory. He found companionship in God himself.

Another cause of discouragement is the wickedness of others. Jeremiah said, "Oh that my head were waters, and mine eyes a fountain of tears, that I might weep day and night for the slain of the daughter of my people!" (Jeremiah 9:1).

He had grown tired of speaking to no avail. He preached and preached, but nobody listened. He exhorted, and nobody obeyed. He cried, and nobody wanted to listen or be helped. This man of God, trying to live a godly life in an evil world, became so discouraged that he wanted to dwell in the wilderness far away from any people.

Jeremiah may not have felt such terrible discouragement had he taken the long view of things. Had he done so, he may have walked around with a smile amid all the iniquity rather than be discouraged.

For over 2,600 years, Jeremiah's book has been a blessing to the world. He gave his testimony, and it seemed to fall on stony ground. But really it didn't. It fell on fruitful soil, which led to many centuries of people being blessed by it.

Keep living for God, continue giving your testimony whenever you can, and don't get discouraged because of the wickedness of others. Always obey God regardless of your circumstances.

Wickedness is spreading worldwide, and there's no place where it doesn't exist. If you find yourself in the midst of great wickedness, don't be discouraged. Our Lord walked among evil men, but Jesus lived, gave of himself, did His holy work, and then said, "I have glorified thee on the earth: I have finished the work which thou gavest me to do" (John 17:4). And Paul said, "I have fought a good fight, I have finished my course, I have kept the faith" (2 Timothy 4:7).

Jeremiah's testimony is still going on today, and we're still drawing consolation from his book. You also can continue to be a testimony for those around you, committing your life to the Lord despite the discouragement that can come from living in this world. And He will see that not one of your tears will be anything less than immortal, for God keeps your prayers in His bottle up in heaven (see Psalm 56:8).

I used to think that when people died, their prayers died. But that's not the case. The truth is that our prayers are preserved in heaven, not kept on ice but before the throne of Almighty God.

When I put all of my discouragement on the table, there is only one cure for it really. That cure is obedience to the Lord. We need to ask God to give us the strength and the faith to follow Him and obey His Word in times of discouragement. Our commitment to obedience is the key that unlocks the prison of discouragement.

Heavenly Father, I praise Thee today for the grace and strength You give me to overcome all elements of discouragement in my life. I bow before Thee in obedience and thank Thee for Thy love and mercy. In Jesus' name I pray, amen.

I Will Follow Thee

I will follow Thee, my Savior,
Wheresoe'er my lot may be;
Where Thou goest I will follow,
Yes, my Lord, I'll follow Thee.

I will follow Thee, my Savior,
Thou didst shed Thy blood for me;
And though all men should forsake Thee,
By Thy grace I'll follow Thee.

Though the road be rough and stormy,
Trackless as the foaming sea,
Thou hast trod this way before me,
And I gladly follow Thee.

Though 'tis lone and dark and dreary,
Cheerless though my path may be,
If Thy voice I hear before me,
Fearlessly I'll follow Thee.

Though I meet with tribulation,
Sorely tempted though I be,
I remember Thou wast tempted,
And rejoice to follow Thee.

Though Thou leadest through afflictions,
Poor, forsaken though I be,
Thou wast destitute, afflicted,
And I only follow Thee.

James L. Elginburg

9

Captivity Rescued through Obedience

Ye have not chosen me, but I have chosen you, and ordained you, that ye should go and bring forth fruit, and that your fruit should remain: that whatsoever ye shall ask of the Father in my name, he may give it you.

John 15:16

Let's explore now the idea of captivity in the life of the Christian, as captivity is a reality for the human race. We read in the Old Testament of the captivity of the Israelites in Egypt and how God rescued them through His servant Moses. And we can point to many examples of this same type of situation in our own culture today.

Picture a young woman who wants to get married when she's a girl and thinks it's nothing but roses: a great husband, a big house, and a nice car. But she discovers something else once she's married and the children arrive. They're wonderful children, and she loves them, but they can be terribly hard on the nerves. Her husband is off working, so the children are in her hands, and the family isn't rich enough to hire a nanny. Though the kids are angels at times, they have a strange way of acting, as if they had come from another planet. This wife and mother finds herself "captivated" but not in the good sense of the word.

It's all right in the beginning and so she puts up with it, but then week follows week, then the months turn into years, and she still has no release. She is captive to the children, cooking for them, blowing their noses, combing their hair, washing faces, pulling them down from places they've been climbing. And of course there's the constant cleaning and the laundry to keep up with. Then one morning she wakes up and asks herself, *Why did I get married and have children?* She feels as though she's in prison and can't get out. She doesn't know what to do.

Likewise, employees can find themselves feeling as if they are being held captive. They go to work, doing the same thing day in and day out as if they're slaves, with their bosses pushing them around, telling them what to do and how to do it. Then one day it all becomes too much, and they tell themselves, *I'm going to quit; I can't take this anymore.* Then they think some more and remember that if they do quit, they may not be able to get another job for a while. Quitting could damage their careers. So they conclude that they have no choice but to stick with their jobs and keep on going.

I could go on and list several other examples of people who, for whatever reason, have become captives in their lives and who see no way out of it. We all can become captives to different things and situations and other people.

Ezekiel, in the Old Testament, was being held captive when suddenly the heavens were opened, and he saw visions of God. Then "the word of the LORD came expressly unto Ezekiel . . . and the hand of the LORD was there upon him" (Ezekiel 1:1–3). This didn't happen as he was strolling amidst a flowery garden, but it happened as he was being held prisoner.

So long as we live, as Christians we will belong to a minority group. Remember, both the world and our country are not in the hands of saints; they're in the hands of Adam's fallen race. Even so, we should be the kind of people who always remain hopeful, if not cheerful, because we have Christ, and He has set us free of our chains. And His Word and promises are our constant companions while we live and work.

The Bible says that David was "a man after God's own heart" (Acts 13:22), but then David walked out onto the palace roof one day and saw Bathsheba. After David had sinned in the eyes of the Lord, God sent Nathan to rebuke him. He approached David and told him a story about a rich man and a poor man.

As Nathan shared the story, David grew angry at the rich man. His response can be found in verse 5 of 2 Samuel 12: "And David's anger was greatly kindled against the man; and he said to Nathan, As the LORD liveth, the man that hath done this thing shall surely die."

After David had expressed his anger, Nathan replied in verse 7, "Thou art the man." Nathan, despite being under David's authority, showed his obedience to God in confronting David, for it was God who told Nathan to rebuke the king of Israel—a man who had been blinded by his sin.

81

I believe when the Bible says David was a man after God's own heart, this meant that David had a passion for obedience. No doubt he made a grievous mistake, but when confronted by Nathan about what he'd done, David yielded to God in repentance. In the end, King David returned to his commitment to obeying the Lord.

Isaiah said, "For the LORD God will help me; therefore shall I not be confounded: therefore have I set my face like a flint, and I know that I shall not be ashamed. He is near that justifieth me; who will contend with me? let us stand together: who is mine adversary? let him come near to me. Behold, the LORD God will help me; who is he that shall condemn me? lo, they all shall wax old as a garment; the moth shall eat them up" (Isaiah 50:7–9).

I would urge you to continue on in your obedience to God regardless of the earthly captivity in which you may find yourself, remembering that the Father in heaven is forever mindful of you. God knows your name and the number of hairs on your head (see Luke 12:7). And He always hears His children's prayers.

We're called to be good men and women in an evil world, to bear witness for the Lord and His goodness to those who don't yet know Him. Don't ever stop doing this, but keep on giving that witness with forbearance and love until God calls you home to be with Him. Until then, obey His voice, thanking God that you're able to share His Word and the gospel message, offering hope and salvation through Jesus Christ to the world's captives.

The little flowers that couldn't come out before will begin to appear. Our little crocuses begin to grow. They are more than growing; they're blooming. Inside your heart you'll be fragrant, and the people will turn their noses in your direction and ask, "Where's that sweet fragrance coming from?" That sweet fragrance will be you because you have cultivated the right spirit.

Yes, our captivity is real, and each of us must face our own captivity. We can only be released from it through our individual obedience to God and His voice. That is our great challenge. We cannot face our captivity by ourselves. Rather, we need to surrender entirely to the Lord and in all things be obedient to His Word.

My captivity is not your captivity, and yours is not mine. You need to understand your captivity from God's point of view, and in order for you to deal with the captivity you find yourself in, you must go to the Word of God and see what He has to say to you. Then you must look to God, confess your sin, and seek His forgiveness and help with obeying His call on your life. God will surely lead you out of your prison if you march on in obedience.

Throughout my years as a Christian I have noticed that the more I grow in the grace and knowledge of God, the more I am given to confession of sin. I confess to what I did not know was sin years before. And as I grow I find that obedience to God's Word is the only resource I need to get out of the spiritual hole I find myself in. When we are willing to humble ourselves and accept our captivity and seek deliverance from God, He will respond in a way that will bring joy to our hearts.

Oftentimes our circumstances don't change much on the outside, yet our hearts change on the inside and in such a way that we begin to view our lives and situations through the merciful eyes of God.

Heavenly Father, I come to You with joy in my heart because as I yield to You in obedience, You respond to me with gifts of deliverance I never thought possible. I praise You for leading me through my places of captivity and into Your joy. Thank You for the freedom I have in You. In Jesus' name I pray, amen.

O Troubled Soul, Beneath the Rod

O troubled soul, beneath the rod
Thy Father speaks—be still, be still;
Learn to be silent unto God,
And let Him mold thee to His will.

Be still, O troubled soul, be still;
Fear not, thy Father's arms enfold thee.
Take up thy cross, lay down thy will;
Be silent unto God, and let Him mold thee.

O anxious soul, lay down thy load,
Oh, hear His voice, He speaks to thee,
"Be still and know that I am God,
And cast thy every care on Me."

O fearful soul, be still, be still,
Be of good cheer; has He not said,
"I will be with you, fear no ill,
'Tis I, 'tis I, be not afraid"?

O praying soul, be still, be still,
He cannot break His plighted word;
Sink down into His blessed will,
And wait in patience on the Lord.

O waiting soul, be still, be strong,
And though He tarry, trust and wait;
Doubt not, He will not wait too long,
Fear not, He will not come too late.

Albert B. Simpson

10

Our Obedience in a Fallen World

That I may know him, and the power of his resurrection, and the fellowship of his sufferings, being made conformable unto his death; If by any means I might attain unto the resurrection of the dead. Not as though I had already attained, either were already perfect: but I follow after, if that I may apprehend that for which also I am apprehended of Christ Jesus.

Philippians 3:10–12

I love the Bible more than any other book in the world. I have a library full of books that I have read, and some of them I've read quite a few times. But there is no book in my library that comes anywhere near the significance of my Bible.

I spend time reading and studying the Bible every day and ask the Holy Spirit to speak to me through the Word of God. And in my opinion, the most important verse in the Bible is Genesis 1:1, which says, "In the beginning God created the heaven and the earth." Everything in the universe is the result of God bringing it into existence by His own hand.

Moreover, when God created heaven and earth, He created all the creatures that inhabit them. He put together specific environments that determine the kind of life each creature will have in that environment.

I like to go bird-watching once in a while, and it's interesting to see how birds prosper in their various environments with the gifts and skills God gave them. Some birds have nests at the very top of the trees, almost without regard for their own safety. This is because these birds are in their own environment there, right where they should be, and they know by a God-given instinct just how they are to live.

Consider the fish swimming about in a lake or stream. The water is the fish's environment, and that environment determines the kind of life that fish will have. If you pull that fish out of the water, it cannot survive and dies very quickly. So long as the fish remain in the environment they were created to exist in, they live healthy lives where they can thrive and happily swim along.

I could go on and on about every creature on earth and how all of them survive in the environment God created for them, and how taking them out of that environment challenges their existence. These creatures are living the life for which they were made, a life that God himself made for them.

Let us now apply this concept to humanity. God created Adam and Eve and placed them in the Garden of Eden. That was their environment, and that was where they were to discover who and what they were. So long as they remained in their environment designed by God, they were healthy and prosperous. Everything about mankind was there in that environment to make them healthy in all regards.

The creation story shows us that as people our God-given environment is always to be in a state of obedience. God expects unquestioning obedience to Him in everything that we do. That obedience then unfolds for us all that God created us for.

It's hard for us today to imagine the environment of the Garden of Eden, where God placed Adam and Eve to live and to commune with Him. Everything about it was perfect, and it was in that environment that Adam and Eve discovered who they were.

In Genesis 1:26, we read, "And God said, Let us make man in our image, after our likeness: and let them have dominion over the fish of the sea, and over the fowl of the air, and over the cattle, and over all the earth, and over every creeping thing that creepeth upon the earth."

The environment for Adam and Eve in the Garden of Eden was for them to have dominion over all of God's creation, to act as stewards of His creation. Though I'm not certain what it was God meant by this, I'm sure Adam understood it and fulfilled it perfectly.

Later, we read in Genesis 2:15–17, "And the Lord God took the man, and put him into the garden of Eden to dress it and to keep it. And the Lord God commanded the man, saying, Of every tree of the garden thou mayest freely eat: But of the tree of the knowledge of good and evil, thou shalt not eat of it: for in the day that thou eatest thereof thou shalt surely die."

The one condition for Adam and Eve in their environment of the Garden of Eden was simply obedience, and there was only one specific thing they had to obey that came from the Lord. And when they disobeyed God's commandment, they immediately lost their identity.

The serpent approached Eve to challenge her obedience: "Now the serpent was more subtil than any beast of the field which the LORD God had made. And he said unto the woman, Yea, hath God said, Ye shall not eat of every tree of the garden?" (Genesis 3:1).

Up to this point, Adam and Eve lived in a perfect environment and had no reason to question God. All their needs were completely met. And then Satan came along and said, "Yea, hath God said?" In other words, Satan suggested to Eve, "Are you sure that's what God said, and are you sure that's what God meant?"

This one act of disobedience took away from humanity that perfect environment found in the Garden of Eden. And ever since this first act of rebellion against the Creator God, human beings have been living in an environment that challenges obedience to God in every way.

So Adam and Eve disobeyed one commandment of the Lord, and it cost them and, by extension, us as well, everything. You may keep ninety-nine commandments, but the commandment you disobey will affect just as much the environment God has established for you in Christ.

The significant consequence of the disastrous fall in the Garden of Eden is that many people and churches are still to this day facing a spiritual identity crisis. By that I mean they do not understand or appreciate their environment in Christ apart from the discipline of obedience.

That is our environment as Christians.

David said in Psalm 17:8, "Keep me as the apple of the eye, hide me under the shadow of thy wings." Here David is expressing his environment in God. He's saying that if we fully understand our true environment under God's protection, we have nothing to fear. Our obedience to God is unchallenged by the world—that is, the world may try to distract us and get us to look away from God, but our obedience to the Lord overrides that challenge with its empty distractions and allurements.

There are many things I cannot do but that God has not required me to do. But there is one thing I can do, and that is to obey His commandments. It may be hard at times, but it is possible for me to obey God no matter the circumstance, as He promises to provide a way of escape whenever we're tempted to disobey Him.

When the serpent came up against Eve, she had the possibility and power to reject his proposal and obey God. But she chose sin instead. Like Eve, our disobedience robs us of what God has for us. Disobedience robs us of our environment in Christ.

In Romans 1:20–22, the apostle Paul says something rather interesting: "For the invisible things of him from the creation of the world are clearly seen, being understood by the things that are made, even his eternal power and Godhead; so that they are without excuse: Because that, when they knew God, they glorified him not as God, neither were thankful; but became vain in their imaginations, and their foolish heart was darkened. Professing themselves to be wise, they became fools. . . ."

Adam and Eve, because of their disobedience, lost their identity in their Creator. At the same time, they lost the perfect environment He had specially made for them. And now all of humanity, having followed suit by choosing sin, is fallen as well. Our hearts are filled with a vast emptiness. We were created to know God, but chose not to.

But, unlike the angels, we are invited by God to return to our true environment of obedience and enjoy communion with Him once again. Why did God abandon forever the angels who rebelled along with Lucifer?

It says in 2 Peter 2:4, "For if God spared not the angels that sinned, but cast them down to hell, and delivered them into chains of darkness, to be reserved unto judgment. . . ." God abandoned those angels because they were never made in His image. They were made physically capable of moral and spiritual perception, but they were not created in God's own image.

Human beings, on the other hand, are expressly made in the image of God himself, and so He offers each of us a chance to be rescued or redeemed. The Bible teaches that we believers are in Christ, who is the image of the invisible God, the brightness of His glory.

The Church fathers proclaimed, "We believe in one Lord, Jesus Christ, the only Son of God, eternally begotten of the Father, God from God, Light from Light, true God from true God, begotten not made, one in being with the Father. Through him all things were made."

The Bible teaches us that it is "in him [Christ] we live, and move, and have our being" (Acts 17:28). Jesus Christ was not only a reflector of deity, although He certainly was that. He was not only a revealer of deity, although he was that. He was and is and always has been the Light of Light, God of God, begotten and not created.

Jesus Christ is the perfect environment in which we are to live and breathe and worship forever. Jesus is just as much God as the Father and the Holy Spirit, and we were created by the Triune God to be in communion with Him every day we live.

Heavenly Father, each day I learn more about my walk with Your Son, the Lord Jesus Christ. While I have much further to go, I'm going to trust the Holy Spirit to direct me every step of the way. I pledge to You my obedience, so that You can take me to where you want me to be. I pray this in the wonderful name of Jesus, amen.

Have You Any Room for Jesus?

Have you any room for Jesus,
He who bore your load of sin?
As He knocks and asks admission,
Sinner, will you let Him in?

Room for Jesus, King of Glory!
Hasten now, His Word obey.
Swing the heart's door widely open;
Bid Him enter while you may.

Room for pleasure, room for business;
But for Christ, the Crucified,
Not a place that He can enter,
In the heart for which He died?

Room and time now give to Jesus;
Soon will pass God's day of grace—
Soon your heart left cold and silent,
And your Savior's pleading cease.

                                   D. W. Whittle

11

The Key to Knowing
the Father's Heart Is Obedience

*That the God of our Lord Jesus Christ, the Father of
glory, may give unto you the spirit of wisdom and
revelation in the knowledge of him. . . .*

Ephesians 1:17

In the animal kingdom, all creatures live according to their
natural instincts, which generally are correct. If they follow their instincts, all will be well. They thrive by obeying
instincts that they have little control over.

The people of the world also live by obeying their instincts, but because of sin and rebellion against God, those
instincts are unhealthy. We can see this all around us, and
sadly it has seeped into the Church as well.

Many of us operate by instinct alone, and that never pleases God, which is why today's Christians know Christ so little. The key to knowing Christ and the Father is obedience. The Scriptures make it quite clear that a relationship with God is predicated on obedience to His Word.

The apostle Peter said, "But grow in grace, and in the knowledge of our Lord and Saviour Jesus Christ. To him be glory both now and for ever. Amen" (2 Peter 3:18). Thus our relationship with Christ is a progressive experience. One of the most exciting things about my walk with the Lord is discovering something about Him I did not know before.

The reason we can always continue to grow in our knowledge of the Lord is because nobody can know everything about the infinite, Almighty God; such a thing is entirely impossible for finite beings such as ourselves.

If God does not give you God, He is giving you thorns instead of bread. If He gives you a garden without giving you himself, He's just giving you an empty garden. If He gives you rain without giving you himself, that rain will destroy you.

God wants to give us himself, but the modern Church seems to be more focused on getting benefits from God. If you published a book explaining ways to get things from God, you are sure to sell a lot of copies of that book—many have done so. In fact, many people think that's the way to bring more people into the Church.

Wanting to get something out of God instead of wanting God himself is the greatest blight that rests upon the Church today. But the sovereign God wants to be loved for himself; He wants to be appreciated and worshiped for himself. And He wants us to know that when we have Him, we have all the rest. Jesus said, "But seek ye first the kingdom of God, and his righteousness; and all these things shall be added unto you" (Matthew 6:33).

Why does God forgive our sin? He forgives sin because sin is what stands between Him and us; our sin is what separates us from Him.

Why does God pour out his Spirit on us? It's so that the Spirit will fill us with His holy presence and power, cleansing us and removing from our hearts all that is not of God and throwing it away.

Why does God answer our prayers? It's so that He might increase our faith and trust in Him. And it's so that He might unveil His will to us and show us how to live in accordance with His Word.

And why has God given us the Scriptures? The purpose of the Bible is to lead us to His beloved Son, Jesus Christ.

Many people speak of the deeper life without truly understanding it. The deeper life is found only in Jesus Christ. As we delve deeper into the knowledge of the Triune God, we will find ourselves in His presence more and more. It's less about us and more about God. Our obedience, then, is the key that unlocks this door, leading us to experience God on a more intimate level.

For we must always be seeking to know the Lord more, and anything that keeps us from knowing Him is the enemy. If there's a distance between you and God, that distance is your enemy. If there's an ambition between you and Him, that ambition is the enemy. If there's a defeat you once suffered that you've allowed to get you down and stand between you and God, that then is your enemy. Put your past failures behind you and press on in faith. Trust God to give you the strength to do so.

Similarly, if there's a victory you won in the past that stands between you and the Lord, you must put that victory behind you too. Keep in mind there are new acts of obedience before you that will lead you forward into the heart of God, the victories you have yet to experience.

Resist the urge to focus on both your mistakes and your victories. Doing so will only serve to hinder you from moving deeper into the knowledge of God. Our obedience not only opens a new door into God's heart but it closes an old door.

Sometimes I want to know all that Paul knew. I want to know what God revealed to him so that I might have the faith and courage to rise up and put under my feet anything that might prevent me from growing in the knowledge of God.

If we want to penetrate deeper into the heart of God, it will only be because of our obedience to His Word. Every day we need to seek a new act of obedience that we can present before God. By obeying His Word, we begin to understand a little bit more of who He is. And we will never get to the end of this path; it's one we will travel forever.

God is so big that we could never, throughout all eternity, come to know everything there is to know about Him. Yet little by little, as we trust Him and obey His Word, we go deeper and deeper into His heart of love. As we get into His heart, several things happen.

First, we slowly but surely come to understand more about God, more about His character and His grace. What is it precisely that God has revealed about himself that He wants you to remember going forward? I'd encourage you to walk with Him on that path, praying and listening to the Holy Spirit. As a result, you will go deeper in your relationship with God.

Second, get to know more about yourself. The Bible says we were created in God's own image and after His likeness. Therefore, if we are to understand ourselves for who we are in Him, then we must seek to know the Lord better—through God's Word, in prayer and meditation. And we can only come to know God through intentional acts of obedience.

Heavenly Father, I seek to know Thee more and more each day. I give myself to Thee and open up my heart, so that You can take complete possession of my life. I want to know and to trust You like I've never known and trusted You before. In Jesus' name I pray, amen.

Deeper and Deeper

Into the heart of Jesus
Deeper and deeper I go,
Seeking to know the reason
Why He should love me so—
Why He should stoop to lift me
Up from the miry clay,
Saving my soul, making me whole,
Though I had wandered away.

Into the will of Jesus
Deeper and deeper I go,
Praying for grace to follow,
Seeking His way to know;
Bowing in full surrender
Low at His blessed feet,
Bidding Him take, break me and make,
Till I am molded and meet.

Into the cross of Jesus
Deeper and deeper I go,
Following through the garden,
Facing the dreaded foe;
Drinking the cup of sorrow—
Sobbing with broken heart,
"O Savior, help! dear Savior, help!
Grace for my weakness impart."

Into the joy of Jesus
Deeper and deeper I go,
Rising, with soul enraptured,
Far from the world below;
Joy in the place of sorrow,
Peace in the midst of pain,
Jesus will give, Jesus will give—
He will uphold and sustain.

Into the love of Jesus
Deeper and deeper I go,
Praising the One who brought me
Out of my sin and woe;
And through eternal ages
Gratefully I shall sing,
"Oh, how He loved! Oh, how He loved!
Jesus, my Lord and my King!"

Oswald J. Smith

12

Strengthened by Our Obedience

The word that came to Jeremiah from the LORD, saying,
Stand in the gate of the LORD's house, and proclaim
there this word, and say, Hear the word of the LORD,
all ye of Judah, that enter in at these gates to worship
the LORD. Thus saith the LORD of hosts, the God of
Israel, Amend your ways and your doings, and I will
cause you to dwell in this place.

Jeremiah 7:1–3

An important question for every Christian to consider is,
Will I continue to grow in Him? God does not want anyone
to perish, to become weak or to lose heart, and we are told
in the Scriptures that our Christian lives are not in jeopardy.
So salvation is not at risk, but what about our spiritual
growth and maturity?

The first thing we must do to foster growth is to put ourselves in the way of God's blessing. It is a great error to think

of God's grace as being like magic, bestowed on us as a kind of windfall that comes suddenly and unexpectedly.

We must remember that God is intelligent, and He made us intelligent, which means His dealings with us are on an intellectual level as well as on a spiritual level. The grace of God does not leap around haphazardly, and it's not something we can have now and then lose tomorrow.

God has laid down certain conditions, and they're not hard to understand. To be blessed by God, we have to put ourselves in the path of God's blessing and grace through obedience to Him. Then, after putting yourself in the path of God's grace, let repentance do its healing work in your heart.

Keep on repenting if necessary. Too often we are impatient to get our repenting over with so that we can move on. Instead, allow God to complete the work to your inner life that needs to be done, trusting the Holy Spirit to cleanse your heart and make you whole.

Penitence includes sorrow and remorse for what you've done or failed to do. We're sorry we're such poor Christians, that we're not as faithful or forgiving as we should be, that we're so coldhearted toward others.

We wish to be more like Paul, who, never thinking he had arrived, said, "Brethren, I count not myself to have apprehended: but this one thing I do, forgetting those things which are behind, and reaching forth unto those things which are before, I press toward the mark for the prize of the high calling of God in Christ Jesus" (Philippians 3:13–14).

Be sorry, and if you do not feel sorry, then pray for a spirit of true repentance. Do not excuse your sin; don't name it something else or try to explain it away. Instead, call it what God calls it: sin, transgression, trespass, iniquity, wickedness.

Take a little time off to be alone with God. Most people today never get alone. It's as if they always need to be in a crowd, among others, and it seems they're the happiest when the group is being led by someone who keeps them always entertained and laughing.

Sit down somewhere outside that is quiet and without distractions. Take in the land, the flowers and trees, the sky and the clouds drifting by. Meditate on the Lord, reciting in your head some verses of Scripture you can remember.

Or open your Bible and read a few verses to get yourself in the right frame of mind. Now take in the vast world around you that He created, the immensity of it all. Listen for the "still small voice" of the Holy Spirit within you. This is a step of obedience that invites God's presence in quiet moments and gives your soul a chance to connect with Him.

Let me also encourage you to think, for God needs sanctified, holy thinkers. God expects us to use that gray matter in our heads. Let us strive, then, to be thoughtful, meditative Christians. Most of the time God can't get our attention; we are busy doing our own thing. He says, "Attention, please," but is anybody listening? Likely not because we're racing madly on our way to one thing or another, dashing off to meetings or hurrying to get to the next activity, whether at church, home, or somewhere else.

Should we not give ourselves time to become acquainted with our own souls? So many people don't have the slightest idea what kind of person they are because they've never stopped long enough to become acquainted with who they are. Yet if we are to obey God in a way that pleases Him and blesses our lives, we need to know who we are *in Christ.*

We must get better acquainted with ourselves while at the same time ceasing to be careless about the way we're going about our lives—examining ourselves spiritually, our personal habits, our relationships, as well as our actions, speech, and thoughts.

And many of us are being poisoned by the world, and we're hardly aware of it. We're allowing the world to develop our ideas and our perspectives. This kind of carelessness in our ordinary affairs can cause Christians to start cooling off in their spiritual lives. This is a dangerous trend. Our obedience should drive us forward in our relationship with God, and whoever loves the ways of the Lord must put the world and its ways behind them. Every act of obedience changes something in the life of the Christian.

One such act of obedience that leads to growth is to cultivate a deep love for God's people. We ought to be seeking fellowship with our brothers and sisters in the Lord, encouraging them and helping to build up their faith. We ought to love everyone equally, not dividing ourselves into different groups according to our different interests, classes, or ages.

Cultivating generosity is one more aspect that will enhance our obedience to God. If we are not generous toward others, we are not like God, for He is generous. I have three suggestions in this regard that I apply to my life that I want to challenge you with:

First, vow to possess nothing. If you have something, use it, but don't *possess* it. Ask God to deliver you from materialism. This can be a challenge among Christians today, those who have aligned with a culture that tells them they deserve nice things, that possessing such things will make them happy. This is a lie.

Second, vow never to pass on injurious rumors you hear about others. Don't be someone who listens to or spreads gossip. Much damage is done because of this practice, and so it's a serious matter in the eyes of the Lord.

Third and last, vow never to take to heart the praise of others. Instead, give God all the glory for any and all achievements. If you vow before God never to take honor for yourself, honoring Him instead, you'll grow in grace and in the knowledge of Jesus Christ. .

We must keep on walking in the way of the cross, amending our ways alongside God's saints, following in the way of holiness and humility before God. If you're faithful in doing this, not only will you hold the ground you took this week by being obedient but you will go even higher. Again, every act of obedience changes something for good in the Christian's life.

Finally, always remain where the grace of Jesus resides, and your obedience will blossom like never before. Jesus said, "Now ye are clean through the word which I have spoken unto you. Abide in me, and I in you" (John 15:3–4).

Heavenly Father, I come into Your presence with great expectation. That expectation has everything to do with who You are and how You want to reveal Yourself to me. I surrender myself completely so that I might know You as You deserve to be known. In Jesus' name I pray, amen.

Jesus Calls Us, O'er the Tumult

Jesus calls us o'er the tumult
Of our life's wild, restless sea;
Day by day his sweet voice sounding,
Saying, "Christian, follow me."

Jesus calls us from the worship
Of the vain world's golden store,
From each idol that would keep us,
Saying, "Christian, love me more."

In our joys and in our sorrows,
Days of toil and hours of ease,
Still he calls, in cares and pleasures,
"Christian, love me more than these."

Jesus calls us—By your mercies,
Savior, may we hear your call,
Give our hearts to your obedience,
Serve and love you best of all.

Cecil F. Alexander

13

The Faith Element in Obedience

And a certain man was there, which had an infirmity thirty and eight years. When Jesus saw him lie, and knew that he had been now a long time in that case, he saith unto him, Wilt thou be made whole? The impotent man answered him, Sir, I have no man, when the water is troubled, to put me into the pool: but while I am coming, another steppeth down before me. Jesus saith unto him, Rise, take up thy bed, and walk. And immediately the man was made whole, and took up his bed, and walked: and on the same day was the sabbath.

John 5:5–9

When Jesus said to the man at the pool, "Rise, take up thy bed, and walk," this must be understood as a command. Of course, what Jesus commands here was impossible and unimaginable, as this man cannot get up, much less take up his bed, and yet the Lord commanded him to do both.

This man was suffering from a chronic illness or disability, and he had been in that state for thirty-eight years. His muscles had likely atrophied, his body in a kind of rigor mortis, and so for him to get up suddenly after so many years of lying flat, pick up his bed, and walk away was beyond his comprehension. No one who was there, including him, would ever have dreamed he could do it. Anybody looking on would have said, "Impossible."

We don't know what exactly was wrong with this man, but it must have been quite serious for him to be left helplessly on his back for thirty-eight years. One thing is for sure: whatever it was this man suffered from, he couldn't get out of it. He was utterly powerless.

Had Jesus not come along, the man would likely have continued to be stuck right where he was, eventually dying there. Jesus Christ, however, because of who He is, could speak the impossible and unimaginable to the man, "Get up and walk," for out of His words flow unspeakable power.

A little later, Jesus said, "It is the spirit that quickeneth; the flesh profiteth nothing: the words that I speak unto you, they are spirit, and they are life" (John 6:63). God's words, therefore, are living words.

God's words are creative words as well. In the beginning, when darkness was upon the face of the deep, God said, "Let there be light, and there was light. God divided the light from the darkness. And God called the light Day, and the darkness he called Night. God said, Let the waters under the heaven be gathered together unto one place, and let the dry land appear: and it was so. And God said, Let the earth bring forth grass, the herb yielding seed, and the fruit tree yielding fruit after his kind, whose seed is in itself, upon the earth: and it was so" (see Genesis 1).

Whenever God speaks, always there is an inherent, indescribable power accompanying His words. So when the Lord Jesus Christ commanded the man to "rise, take up thy bed, and walk," there was something in Jesus' voice that enabled the man to obey Him—just as when the Triune God said in the book of Genesis, "Let there be," and there was. He spoke His words to heal the man, just as by His words He formed the world and made the stars to shine.

Thus the Word of the living God is powerful and creative beyond all human comprehension, and when God Almighty speaks, it carries supernatural, life-giving power. As the Lord said to the man, "Get up and walk," so much power was released in that instant, it was not difficult for the impossible and unimaginable to be made possible, and become a reality in the sight of all who were present.

Our obedience connects us to this same mysterious, creative power.

But notice that a response from the man was required in order for Jesus' power to be released, a response that included equal measures of faith, humility, and obedience in submission to God's will. Immediately, then, he was made whole, and so the man rose, took up his bed, and walked. The ability to obey was connected to the decision to obey. I realize how simple this sounds, but we need to get ahold of the principle here, that the ability to do the impossible comes with the decision to obey God's voice, His words to us.

Jesus said, "Get up and walk," which for this man was impossible, but again there was power in His words to make the impossible possible and to bring to pass what could never happen naturally in a million years. And yet a decision also had to be made in the heart of the man who had lain there for thirty-eight years.

When a soul encounters God like this, something mysterious occurs that we might call the role of the unknown wherein God's actions remain obscure and out of our hands. It is then the sovereign God enters the scene with His all-creative work, His life-bringing work, and He steps in and performs a bewildering act that the soul cannot understand.

The Church as a whole needs to realize and experience this powerful mystery, much like the helpless man heard a voice telling him to do what he couldn't do. His mind couldn't understand or analyze it, and he could not know what was happening. Yet his will responded to the command of Jesus, and he made the decision to obey the voice, even though reason told him the whole thing was impossible.

The man's long history of thirty-eight years dictated that there was no way he could get up and walk. But in that moment between impotence and bounding health, between being lost and being saved, something was stirring, a mysterious working of the sovereign God, doing for a man that which he could not understand.

So too there is a precise moment between the saved and the lost when each soul is called upon to pay close attention, to consider the creative word that has been spoken. We are told to "get up and walk," and yet we're lying there powerless. That's when faith must do something. Faith has to leap across the gap and believe in Christ regardless of what appears on the surface to be impossible and unimaginable.

The man lying at the pool knew for a fact he couldn't get up and walk under his own power. He had managed to talk loud enough to be heard by Jesus, but that was all. Then he heard Jesus' commands to him, "Rise, take up thy bed, and walk," and this man could see he had nothing to lose. That was when a divine realization settled over this man. Perhaps he told himself, "If I continue to lie here, I'll likely die and soon." And in the midst of the unknown, he believed. He got up and walked. Where before there was helplessness, now there is strength. Where before he was unable to move, he can now stand up on his own two feet and stride forward—all because there was a right response in his heart to the creative words of the living Christ.

Heavenly Father, I had no power to do anything on my own, but You came along and invited me to follow You. Give me the strength and faith I need to obey Your voice as I should for Your glory. In Jesus' name I pray, amen.

Jesus, I Come

Out of my bondage, sorrow and night,
Jesus, I come, Jesus, I come;
Into thy freedom, gladness, and light,
Jesus, I come to thee.
Out of my sickness into thy health,
Out of my want and into thy wealth,
Out of my sin and into thyself,
Jesus, I come to thee.

Out of my shameful failure and loss,
Jesus, I come, Jesus, I come;
Into the glorious gain of thy cross,
Jesus, I come to thee.
Out of earth's sorrows into thy balm,
Out of life's storms and into thy calm,
Out of distress to jubilant psalm,
Jesus, I come to thee.

Out of unrest and arrogant pride,
Jesus, I come, Jesus, I come;
Into thy blessed will to abide,
Jesus, I come to thee.
Out of myself to dwell in thy love,
Out of despair into raptures above,
Upward for aye on wings like a dove,
Jesus, I come to thee.

Out of the fear and dread of the tomb,
Jesus, I come, Jesus, I come;
Into the joy and light of thy home,
Jesus, I come to thee.
Out of the depths of ruin untold,
Into the peace of thy sheltering fold,
Ever thy glorious face to behold,
Jesus, I come to thee.

William T. Sleeper

14

Hearing Is Critical
to Obedience

Again, he limiteth a certain day, saying in David, To day, after so long a time; as it is said, To day if ye will hear his voice, harden not your hearts.

Hebrews 4:7

But be ye doers of the word, and not hearers only, deceiving your own selves. For if any be a hearer of the word, and not a doer, he is like unto a man beholding his natural face in a glass: For he beholdeth himself, and goeth his way, and straightway forgetteth what manner of man he was. But whoso looketh into the perfect law of liberty, and continueth therein, he being not a forgetful hearer, but a doer of the work, this man shall be blessed in his deed.

James 1:22–25

Obedience is essential in the Christian's life, and the key to that obedience is to hear properly, to wait upon God. For if we don't hear what God is saying to us, how might we obey Him?

Often we catch only fragments of what's being said, failing to grasp the full picture. It is this partial understanding that can lead us astray. It's crucial, then, to hear the entire truth. Taking in only a piece of the truth can compromise our obedience.

We must remember that every heresy is built upon a fragment of truth. Heretics take the truth and twist it in the direction they want to go, which is why it is so important that we know all the truth. Oftentimes we hear what the truth is, but then need help comprehending the whole of what's being said, the full conversation.

This can lead to misunderstandings, a common issue among Christians today. They hear parts of the truth, just not the whole story. However, as we open the Word of God and ask the Holy Spirit to illuminate in our hearts the full truth, we're given a new perspective and then obedience follows.

Some Christians believe they are obeying God's Word when they have heard but a portion of it and not the whole thing. They think they are doing the right thing but haven't heard all of the truth being revealed. In our journey with Christ, it is essential that we take in all of His Word.

Picture someone who is hard of hearing. They may hear only a portion of a conversation, become confused, then get upset with someone for saying something they didn't actually say. Many Christians are like this in their understanding of God's Word. They pick and choose Bible verses and come to a completely different conclusion from what the whole

Bible teaches, and so their obedience to His Word is carried out in error, which leads them down the wrong path. That's one of the reasons we have so many different denominations throughout the Christian world. Everyone bases their beliefs on the Word of God, though most of the time they are cherry-picking God's truth, which is the devil's way of dividing God's people.

When I first became a Christian, I was obeying certain things I was taught from the Bible. As I grew older and delved deeper into the Word of God, my obedience began to expand further. I am obeying God today a little different from when I was younger because I have allowed God's Word in all its fullness to enter my heart.

In the Scriptures you will notice different types of hearers. There's the **faithless hearer**. Israel had the gospel preached to them, the apostle Paul tells us, but it did not help them because it wasn't mixed with faith (see Hebrews 4:2). There was insufficient faith in the hearts of the people who heard the gospel. Paul's saying it's possible to believe the right thing but only theologically. We can believe the truth and yet it has little effect on our daily lives. Our obedience must include faith.

There's the **dull hearer**. A dull hearer is someone who becomes bored with what they are hearing. And a lot of boredom or dullness results from hearing something and not doing anything about it. When we don't act on the truth, this also can result in it not having any real effect on our lives.

There's the **critical hearer**. A critical hearer is judgmental. No matter what it is they hear, they are critical about it, and they're only listening really to hear something wrong with it. Maybe the preacher's delivery isn't quite what it should be, or maybe some of the grammar isn't up to correct standards.

Again, whatever it is, this hearer will find something to criticize. This hearer will not come to understand the full truth and therefore their obedience is compromised.

There's the **forgetful hearer**. Satan delights in stealing the seed from the hearer's heart who cannot remember what they were taught to begin with. We cannot be helped by the truth if we've forgotten it, and our obedience is sometimes simply based on our remembering the truth. When we forget certain truths shown to us from God's Word, this will begin to affect how we think and live, the choices we make. And if it's a key truth, you can be sure the devil is going to try his best to wipe it from our memories.

There's the **neglectful hearer**. This hearer has good intentions, but nothing ever happens—that is, no action is taken and so there's no real effect on the person's life. They have a habit of kicking the can down the road time and time again, until the truth they once heard has little or no impact on their lives. Have you ever stopped to think just how much you could have accomplished spiritually had you followed through with what you intended to do?

St. Bernard of Clairvaux has been credited with saying, "The road to hell is paved with good intentions." Keep in mind the passage of Scripture in which Paul and Silas were in prison and facing a trembling jailer, who fell down before the two prisoners and asked, "Sirs, what must I do to be saved?" And Paul answered, "Believe on the Lord Jesus Christ, and thou shalt be saved, and thy house" (see Acts 16:29–31). The jailer had to act immediately upon hearing the Word of the Lord, and so must we today.

Finally, there's the **submissive hearer**. When a submissive hearer is told the truth, they submit to it in its entirety. It's not that they understand everything about that truth, but they do understand it comes from God and so they yield their hearts and their understanding to Him. The submissive hearer says, "Here I am, Lord, ready and willing to hear whatever it is you have to say to me."

How precious is the little time we have left on this earth, and how vital it is in light of the eternal future that lies before each of us. Therefore, we should carefully and thoughtfully consider how we hear God's truth as well as how we read and interpret His truth as revealed to us in the Scriptures.

If we're going to live obediently in our walk with God, we must commit to hearing and receiving *all the truth*, completely. This is the work of the Holy Spirit in our lives as we yield to the Word of God. Hearing the truth rightly will enable us to obey what we may not understand: "For we walk by faith, not by sight" (2 Corinthians 5:7). Our obedience is based on the clarity of our hearing and responding to God's truth, not necessarily on the clarity of our understanding His truth in its entirety.

Whatever it takes for you to hear all of God's truth, whether you fully understand it or not, that is what you must do in faith, trusting Him for the rest. Nothing must come between you and God's truth.

Heavenly Father, I open up my heart today to receive from You the truth that will change my life. I surrender to Your Word entirely and to Your will for me. Give me all that I need to obey You in every respect and guide me, Lord, along the way. In Jesus' name I pray, amen.

O *Word of God Incarnate*

O Word of God incarnate,
O Wisdom from on high,
O Truth, unchanged, unchanging,
O Light of our dark sky,
we praise Thee for the radiance
that from the hallowed page,
a lantern to our footsteps,
shines on from age to age.

The church from her dear Master
received the gift divine,
and still that light she lifteth
o'er all the earth to shine.
It is the golden casket,
where gems of truth are stored;
it is the heav'n-drawn picture
Of Christ, the living Word.

It floateth like a banner
before God's host unfurled;
it shineth like a beacon
above the darkling world.
It is the chart and compass
that o'er life's surging sea,
'mid mists and rocks and quicksands,
still guides, O Christ, to Thee.

O make Thy Church, dear Savior,
a lamp of burnished gold,
to bear before the nations
Thy true light as of old.
O teach Thy wand'ring pilgrims
by this, their path to trace,
'til, clouds and darkness ended,
they see Thee face to face.

William W. How

15

Blessings that Flow from Obedience

Blessed is the man that trusteth in the LORD, *and whose hope the* LORD *is. For he shall be as a tree planted by the waters, and that spreadeth out her roots by the river, and shall not see when heat cometh, but her leaf shall be green; and shall not be careful in the year of drought, neither shall cease from yielding fruit.*

Jeremiah 17:7–8

Obedience to God and His Word is also a critical factor in that it is through obedience that His blessings flow into our lives—that is to say, without our practicing obedience, we cannot and will not receive all that God wants for us.

The key to all this is to place our faith in Jesus Christ alone, who out of His great love bestows upon us the spiritual ability to obey Him. This ability is given to each Christian by God himself to put their trust in His Son, the Lord Jesus, through the power of the Holy Spirit.

Such faith cannot be manufactured; rather, it is received through the Word of God by His grace. And it is by faith that we receive from Him this ability as well as the strength to obey God's voice, especially in areas we as finite beings don't fully understand.

I've discovered in my lifetime that the more I come to know, the more I do not know. Even though I've been a Christian for more than fifty years, there are still many things about God and His Word that I don't understand. Yes, I'm growing in the grace and knowledge of Jesus Christ, and I understand more today than I did ten years ago. But today I will learn something new from God as I obey His Word and trust Him in everything I do.

I can only imagine what my life would be like if it all rested on my intelligence. Sometimes I think I'm really smart, but then God sends something my way that's beyond my intelligence. At that moment, I must confess, I turn my life over to God and let Him control it.

When I do that, I position myself where God wants me to be so that God can flow through me with His blessings. I don't know what the next blessing will be, but I will recognize it when it comes. That's part of what makes the Christian life so exciting. As I have obeyed God, He has sent me blessings I had no idea would ever come my way. The devil wants me to think that I'm not worthy, and of course the devil has something there. Yes, I am not worthy, but obeying God brings me blessing anyway.

In regard to our obedience to God, we should always seek to be where He wants us to be, when He wants us to be there.

God, speaking to His servant Moses, said, "Behold, there is a place by me, and thou shalt stand upon a rock: And it shall come to pass, while my glory passeth by, that I will put thee in a clift of the rock, and will cover thee with my hand while I pass by: And I will take away mine hand, and thou shalt see my back parts: but my face shall not be seen" (Exodus 33:21–23). This passage of Scripture offers us a beautiful illustration of the God-hidden life.

Moses truly was a man of faith who followed God in sacrificial obedience. I've come to believe that such faith-filled followers of God can be placed in four distinct categories:

1) The person of faith as a God-charmed follower of the Lord.

This person lives in the center of the miracle and becomes in essence a true Bible mystic. They feel as though the whole world is theirs.

The God-charmed one sees the miracle, whereas everybody else sees no miracle at all. It is not a sign of senility or a sign that this person has lost their mind when they insist on seeing God or hearing the voice of God in the sigh of the wind or in the roar of a storm.

The God-charmed person finds that they are entirely safe. It was said about Jesus that His hour had not yet come (John 7:30), which was why His enemies couldn't harm Him while He walked and served among them.

There's a similar passage in the Old Testament. When Elisha was in the city of Dothan, his servant became frightened because the king had sent a great host with chariots, horses, and soldiers against him (see 2 Kings 6:13–23). The young, inexperienced man hadn't known that Elisha lived a charmed life and inhabited a perpetual miracle. Excited, he came running to his master and said, "Alas, my master! how shall we do?"

The old man said, "Fear not: for they that be with us are more than they that be with them" (2 Kings 6:16). And the Lord opened the eyes of the young man, and he looked at his surroundings.

Elisha prayed, "Smite this people, I pray thee, with blindness." And they became temporarily blind, and he led them into Samaria and captured them. These two men led the whole army. The young man said, "Father, what shall we do? Kill them?" "No," he said. "Give them something to eat and send them back." Elisha had inhabited a miracle and so he didn't wish to hurt anyone.

At last Elisha said, "'Now, Lord, let them see.' And every man saw. They were in Samaria captured."

Therefore, if a person obeys God, and they go where God sends them, they are part of a charmed circle and quite safe until their work on earth is done, until God is ready for them to come home to be with Him in heaven. God will always defend the faith-filled person who is following Him, who's actively obeying His will.

The preacher Lucius Bunyan Compton, who came from North Carolina, was once sued by a rich man for something for which he wasn't to blame. But this man had influence on his side.

"Why do you not get witnesses to defend you?" the rich man asked Compton. "I can't," Compton answered. "God won't let me. All God lets me do is pray."

So he prayed down to the wire. Eventually he was tried in court, and they charged everything against Compton.

He stayed calm, waiting on God in prayer. A few hours before the court trial ended, Compton received a call. "Please come here and pray for a man who is desperately ill."

He hurried to where the sick man was, and it turned out the man was the very one who was suing him. Compton got down on his knees beside the bed and prayed for the ailing man. He was then healed, and afterward the man called the suit off.

God defends His people when they belong to this charmed circle.

2) The person of faith as a God-taught follower of the Lord. "But we speak the wisdom of God in a mystery, even the hidden wisdom, which God ordained before the world unto our glory . . ." (1 Corinthians 2:7). And that wisdom of God sometimes leads in ways we can't comprehend.

A friend shared with me this story about a fellow brother in the Lord. Though the brother didn't have much of an education, he was a deeply spiritual man of God. When he was a young preacher, he was singing on the radio one day when he got a call asking if he would come to a certain home to preach and worship.

He took his guitar, hymnbooks, and a friend, and they drove out to the house. When they arrived, the yard was filled with cars, and the house was full of people sitting around on metal folding chairs.

When he walked inside, they looked at him in confusion. He told them that God had sent him to meet with them, so he passed the hymnbooks around, tuned his guitar, and sang for a while. Then he asked his friend to testify, which he did.

Afterward he started preaching to the gathering of people. When he finished, he collected the hymnbooks and guitar, and he and his friend headed for the car.

Somebody followed him outside and asked, "Would you pray that my sister gets healed?"

He went and did so, then discovered that he had gone to the wrong house. It was a family reunion he had attended, not the home where he'd been asked to come and share in worship. He was a simplehearted man, yet he knew the voice of God when he heard it.

3) The person of faith as a prayerful, instinctive follower of the Lord.

There's a God-given spiritual instinct, which is a hidden mystery among such believers. They often find that God has been speaking to others as they have been praying, saying the same thing He had been speaking to them when in prayer, typically over a considerable period of time. What the Holy Spirit is communicating to them, and how He's directing everyone involved, follows a pattern they all recognize as the hand of God at work.

4) Finally, the person of faith as a privileged follower of the Lord.

It says in 1 Corinthians 2:15–16, "But he that is spiritual judgeth all things, yet he himself is judged of no man. For who hath known the mind of the Lord, that he may instruct him? but we have the mind of Christ."

The Holy Spirit pours into this privileged one the favor of God that has no limit whatsoever. God's grace and mercy are manifested, and it all boils down to their faithful obedience to God.

Heavenly Father, I praise Thee for the richness of Thy grace that You have poured into my life. Thank You for all that You are and all that You've done for me. I want to surrender myself to You every day that I live. In Jesus' name I pray, amen.

Count Your Blessings

When upon life's billows you are tempest tossed,
When you are discouraged, thinking all is lost,
Count your many blessings, name them one by one,
And it will surprise you what the Lord hath done.

Count your blessings, name them one by one;
Count your blessings, see what God hath done;
Count your blessings, name them one by one;
Count your many blessings, see what God hath done.

Are you ever burdened with a load of care?
Does the cross seem heavy you are called to bear?
Count your many blessings, ev'ry doubt will fly,
And you will be singing as the days go by.

When you look at others with their lands and gold,
Think that Christ has promised you His wealth untold;
Count your many blessings, money cannot buy
Your reward in heaven, nor your home on high.

So, amid the conflict, whether great or small,
Do not be discouraged, God is over all;
Count your many blessings, angels will attend,
Help and comfort give you to your journey's end.

Johnson Oatman Jr.

16

In Darkness We Find Obedience

The day is thine, the night also is thine: thou hast prepared the light and the sun.

Psalm 74:16

Those first words are important, "The day is thine, the night also is thine." The night belongs to God as well as the day. The day is universally beloved, while the night is often feared and avoided.

Occasionally, a poet will say something inspiring about the night, such as when Robert Southey wrote, "How beautiful is night! / A dewy freshness fills the silent air; / No mist obscures, nor cloud, nor speck, nor stain, / Breaks the serene of heaven. . . ."

But the human race's instinct is to be repelled by the night and drawn to the day—that is, the physical night and the physical day because we're made for the day. We're not nocturnal creatures, but diurnal. We belong to the day. Throughout the Scriptures, much is made of the idea of day and night. Typically, the day symbolizes the kingdom of God and heaven, righteousness, and everlasting peace, whereas the night symbolizes the reign of sin, destruction, and ultimately hell.

The apostle John states, "God is light, and in him is no darkness at all" (1 John 1:5). In the light of day, we see a number of things we cannot perceive or discern in the pitch-darkness. For instance, light gives us knowledge. A man who stands in pitch-dark night may be within one foot of a cliff over which he could easily stumble to his death. Or the man may be within one foot of his own door and not know it because it takes light to bring knowledge.

Light also enables us to know our way home. A traveler must have light; even a compass is of no help in leading you in the right direction if you haven't the light to *see* the compass.

Just as the sun is the lord of the day, bringing knowledge, perception, and vital information, God is the Lord of the kingdom of light, bringing holiness, justice, wisdom, love, and peace. God calls us into His light.

The most straightforward way to put it is that God calls us from dishonesty to honesty, from moral wickedness to purity, from hate to love, from envy to charity, from lying to truth, and from evil to good. This is elementary, but it is true nonetheless. God's call from the darkness of wickedness to the light of truth and holiness is a constant call to the world and those who have been led astray by their disobedience and sin.

And when the dwellers in darkness come into the light, what a radiance of beauty they see for the first time. What a lifting of the load, what a rolling away of fear, and what an inward well of comfort, joy, and peace there springs up. Simply put, this is conversion.

But after we have been converted a long while, we tend to forget what happened. We begin to take our new situation in the light for granted, like the couple who has been married for several years. The radiance of those first days in the new relationship starts to fade. Every so often we Christians ought to recall the terrible darkness out of which we were rescued, refreshing our souls in worship, thanking God for His glorious light and for our conversion.

Scripture teaches us, then, that the day belongs to God, along with light, holiness, morality, purity, and joy. But the Bible also teaches that the night belongs to God. Here we come to a different meaning of the word *night*; the word seen here is an extension of sorts, borrowed from the ancient world.

As many of God's children can't stand the night, I must explain that by night I do not mean wickedness. Instead, I mean that state of affairs that wickedness has brought to the world, which we all must live in the midst of. We're in it certainly, but we are not part of it. All the evil in the world is right here among us, and it is darkness to the core. It's important to remember, however, that our sovereign, holy God also holds that in His very capable hands.

If there were any part of God's world that He did not have control over, there would soon be a rebellion that would shake the throne on high. As for the sovereign God, the night remains his, and though He has no affinity for the world's wickedness, He's still in control of this world. So the darkness around us is in His hands, as are we all.

There are those of God's children who cannot abide this. They fear the night and wither in the darkness. They are lonely children of the day, and they have never learned the secret and the blessing of the dark night of the soul. God has to leave a light on for them, much like parents leave a little light on at night for their children so that they won't become afraid.

God has to keep some people out of trouble because they are not spiritually strong enough to understand how to overcome it. Yet if they don't experience trouble, they're likely not to mature in their faith and their relationship with Him. So God can't yet expose them to the night, but they won't grow in Him until they have faced the night in faith.

There are others, though, who have learned to walk in darkness in faith—not walking immorally in the darkness, but walking morally and uprightly while living in a dark world. The apostle Paul said, "Holding forth the word of life; that I may rejoice in the day of Christ, that I have not run in vain, neither laboured in vain" (Philippians 2:16). The sovereign God forces even the darkness to serve His will and purposes, and compels the sullen night to discipline His children. Their spiritual maturity depends on it, for it is often in the dead of night that they learn to pray sincerely, to call upon Him when they're feeling alone, afraid, uncertain, or tempted.

We never want it to rain; we want the sun to shine continually. But if the sun shone continually, the earth would be baked beyond all recognition, and all would wither and die. It takes the cool rain, mingled with the warm sun, to produce the earth's vegetation and to nurture the flora and fauna that God has given us so richly to enjoy.

Notice the sharp contrast laid out in 2 Corinthians 4:17–
18, which says, "For our light affliction, which is but for a
moment, worketh for us a far more exceeding and eternal
weight of glory; While we look not at the things which are
seen, but at the things which are not seen: for the things
which are seen are temporal; but the things which are not
seen are eternal."

So there is affliction, but it is light. There is glory, but it
is heavy. There is affliction, but it is for a moment. There is
glory, but it is eternal. If we keep all this in mind, we would
not be afraid of the night, and we wouldn't always need to
plead with God to keep a light burning to prevent us from
whimpering. The night comprises its own unique ministry
and purpose, and this is a blessing to us because it's in the
night that our obedience has its most significant effect.

By night I do not mean sin, but the circumstances in which
we find ourselves in this fallen world: the difficult situation
we're in, the visitation of sickness, the loss of a loved one,
the disappointment of our hopes, and the discouragement
we feel when people fail us. The attacks of the enemy and of
the devil himself coming to us are all darkness at work, and
we're in the midst of it and can't escape it. The Scriptures
and hymns and spiritual songs we share to uplift ourselves
and one another all teach us this.

There is a joy in the fact that the cross is a beautiful thing
to carry and that joy comes in the morning after a night of
weeping. If this is not true, then we ought to quit singing
about it. If it is true, and surely it is, then we ought to start
believing it.

God uses the day with its sun and the night with its darkness. He uses good people with their hope and cheer and evil

people with their persecution and dishonesty. He uses health with its buoyancy and perhaps illness as well. The Church has believed through the centuries that the Lord sometimes chastens His people by allowing them to experience illness (see 1 Corinthians 11). Every time you get a pain, don't accept the idea that pain is the result of your failing the Lord in some way. The Lord may turn that pain into good, deepening and broadening your faith in Him.

When God Almighty turns loose on us the ministry of day and night, of good and bad, of God and the devil himself, He makes the devil work for us. He hitches him up, harnesses him like the dumb donkey that he is, and makes him pull the cart for the saints of God.

God has always done this, and He's still doing it. I don't like the devil, but when he starts roaring and seeking who he may devour, God bottles up his roar and evil plans and makes them work for His kingdom and for the saints of the Most High God. And the winds as they blow and the stars in their courses all fight for the men and women God delights to honor.

Our obedience to God brings all of this together in a way that glorifies and honors Him.

Heavenly Father, I praise Thee for the daylight, and I praise Thee for the night. I confess I sometimes confuse the two, but it is my solemn desire to serve Thee both in the day and through the night in obedience to Your call on my life. In Jesus' name I pray, amen.

I Want to Walk as a Child of the Light

I want to walk as a child of the light.
I want to follow Jesus.
God set the stars to give light to the world.
The star of my life is Jesus.

In him there is no darkness at all.
The night and the day are both alike.
The Lamb is the light of the city of God.
Shine in my heart, Lord Jesus.

I want to see the brightness of God.
I want to look at Jesus.
Clear sun of righteousness, shine on my path,
and show me the way to the Father.

I'm looking for the coming of Christ.
I want to be with Jesus.
When we have run with patience the race,
we shall know the joy of Jesus.

Kathleen Thomerson

17

The Subtle Aspect of Obedience

*Behold, the LORD thy God hath set the land before thee:
go up and possess it, as the LORD God of thy fathers
hath said unto thee; fear not, neither be discouraged.*

Deuteronomy 1:21

I would like to expand on this theme of the ministry and blessing of the night because I think it's important to consider how this affects our obedience to God in various ways. That heartache you've carried around with you and are still carrying, the night of suffering, can help you grow deeper in your faith.

As I reflect back on my life, I must admit there have been many dark times. There were times when I was tempted to give up and quit and go hide somewhere. Thank God I didn't. It was in the darkest times that I learned more about God and my relationship with Him than at any other time in my life. Those dark moments worked to separate me from everything else until all I could focus on was God and His Word.

I certainly don't want to go through dark times again, although it is true that the darkest times I've suffered through were also the best times I experienced with God. They taught me that obedience to God is always worth it. Jesus himself was called "the man of sorrow," as He was well acquainted with grief. So in this chapter I want us to consider some of the ways the night can reveal itself.

To begin with, I think of the story of Abraham, who, in obedience to God, took up a knife to slay "thine only son Isaac, whom thou lovest"—this after God had instructed him to "get thee into the land of Moriah; and offer him [Isaac] there for a burnt offering . . ." (Genesis 22:1–13). As we all know, at the right moment, before it was too late, God stopped Abraham from killing and sacrificing his son. But all the psychological, inward pain of what he'd been commanded to do by God had already taken place within him.

When Abraham responded to God, saying, "Yes, I will slay my son," already he had died in his heart. There was nothing in his life more important than Isaac. He had waited years for the boy to enter his life. Already he was a wounded man, slowly bleeding to death inside, and yet God quickly stanched the wound and healed Abraham and gave him back his son along with everything else, blessing him and making his name great.

At that precise moment, Abraham realized that when he obeyed God, he was putting his whole life into God's hands. God is to be trusted in all things, and no matter the cost personally. Through Abraham all the nations of the earth have been blessed, but first this servant of God had to be tested;

138

he had to experience the sudden settling down of the dark night in the midst of the unknown. I remember a dear old Irish preacher named Robert Cunningham. I never knew how old he was, but he was so thin he couldn't get any thinner. Always while speaking to his congregation, he would look up at the ceiling. Nobody ever knew why. Many criticized him for praying too much and for too long. He once told me, "If the only criticism my friends have against me is that I pray too much, well, that's all right with me."

On the surface, one could say he was a failure. Nobody called him and said, "Brother Cunningham, come and preach to our gathering of five hundred ministers." If they had, he likely would have just stood there staring at the ceiling and talking in a dry way. But God's hand was upon this man's life and ministry. In truth he was a saint who walked closely with God, and then one day God took him home to be with Him.

To you Christians who are struggling in your walk with God, keep in mind that sometimes your failure is the evidence of the hand of God upon your life. We often get all out of shape when it looks as though we're failing. We want to control the outcome and appear successful to everyone around us, but sometimes that's not the way God is leading us. Sometimes He's leading us straight into the ministry of the night.

Jesus died there on the cross, and at that dark moment it looked as if this was the bitter end of a man who had meant well but who didn't know how to handle himself, the tragic result being His own execution at the hands of His captors. Then, three days later, God raised Jesus from the dead, set Him at His right hand, and made His Son the head over all things in heaven and on earth. As the Scripture says, "And hath put all things under his feet, and gave him to be the head over all things to the church, Which is his body, the fulness of him that filleth all in all" (Ephesians 1:22–23). Further, just before issuing the Great Commission, Jesus told His disciples, "All power [authority] is given unto me in heaven and in earth" (Matthew 28:18).

God sent Elijah to go before Ahab and proclaim, "There will be no rain. And when there is no rain, there is no water, and when there is no water, there is no brook" (see 1 Kings 17). So his preaching dried up the brook he was drinking from.

The man who preached his own head off was John the Baptist. He died an apparent failure, and they carried his head on a silver platter and handed it to the bloated old king. What did the people think of John the Baptist? They said it would have been better had he never been born. What a helpless wretch he was.

An overwhelming sense of coldness can affect all of God's children at some point. David of the Old Testament experienced spells of coldness, and he blamed God for them. He went straight to God and said, "Bless me and bring me out of this." He didn't try to blame his predicament on others. Instead, he prayed, "O God, you've turned away from me. Bless me now." And the Lord heard David's prayer and restored him.

Have you ever experienced a cold period that you couldn't seem to escape from? You find yourself overwhelmed, fatigued, weary both in body and soul. Your mind lacks clarity, and your nerves become frazzled. Occasionally, we as Christians go through these periods of coldness and fear when we wonder whether all will ever be well again.

Irishwoman Ann Preston ("Holy Ann") herself went through a long spell of coldness, as did Hannah Whitall Smith, who wrote *The Christian's Secret of a Happy Life*. Such is the case with so many other believers too, those who are not so well-known. A glimpse into our listless hearts often disconcerts us and grieves us so much that we can find no joy for a time.

Yet it is through the cold spells of suffering and penitence and sorrow and loss and failure and tribulation that God takes that which is outward and drives it inward as He works to perfect the soul of each of His children, thereby teaching us to walk by faith and put our trust in Him alone.

Though we must all pass through the dark night of the soul from time to time, all will be well in the end. Ours is a full salvation, and the Lord Jesus promises to guide us by His Spirit as we commit ourselves to keep on obeying His Word no matter our circumstances.

Heavenly Father, my heart at times becomes discouraged because of the darkness of the night. I thank Thee that You are bigger than my sorrows and disappointments. I praise Thee for the joy that comes to me even in the darkest of nights. In Jesus' name I pray, amen.

Through the Love of God Our Savior

Through the love of God our Savior,
all will be well.
Free and changeless is his favor,
all, all is well.
Precious is the blood that healed us,
perfect is the grace that sealed us,
strong the hand stretched forth to shield us,
all must be well.

Though we pass through tribulation,
all will be well.
Ours is such a full salvation,
all, all is well.
Happy, still in God confiding,
fruitful, if in Christ abiding,
holy, through the Spirit's guiding,
all must be well.

We expect a bright tomorrow,
all will be well.
Faith can sing through days of sorrow,
"All, all is well."
On our Father's love relying,
Jesus every need supplying,
in our living, in our dying,
all must be well.

Mary Peters

18

How the Bible Affects Our Obedience

Blessed are the undefiled in the way, who walk in the law of the LORD. Blessed are they that keep his testimonies, and that seek him with the whole heart.

Psalm 119:1–2

Further on in this psalm, David says, "For ever, O LORD, thy word is settled in heaven" (Psalm 119:89). We quote these words quite a lot, but why should they be so priceless to us? I believe it is because they speak of something we do not have and cannot find here on earth: permanence and perpetuity.

The word *permanence* means that something will always be exactly like it is now, and *perpetuity* means it will last on through the centuries. And there's nothing else like this in this world. None of us has seen anything with our eyes or felt anything with our hands that was permanent.

Perhaps you've built yourself a beautiful house, and I don't mind or envy you if you can live in such a charming place. But remember this: there will come a day when the foxes and raccoons will live where that house now stands; the moles will burrow in that place, and you'll go the way of dust and long be forgotten.

Permanence isn't something that belongs to the human race, nor does perpetuity belong to us because *nothing* lasts. Nothing on earth is settled, that is, except for God's Word: "For ever, O LORD, thy word is settled in heaven."

I hold in my hand a beautiful leather-bound Bible. The day will come, however, when the pages of this Bible will yellow, its binding rot away, until the book will fall apart and somebody will toss it into the wastebin. But the promises it contains will endure forever.

Along with my Bible, all else will change and fall apart too as the ages roll on, one after the next. Meanwhile, various peoples throughout the world will be born, live a short while, then die and be lowered into their graves to decay. And all their sadness and laughter shall be silenced. Again, there's nothing on this earth that lasts, save for one thing and one thing only: "For ever, O LORD, thy word is settled in heaven."

The Word of God contains enormous power. We can see evidence of this in His creation, *ex nihilo*, in the book of Genesis, where we find the Creator God speak forth the command, "Let there be . . . ," and there was. And He said, "Let the light come," and it came; and He said, "Let the grass grow," and it grew. God spoke, and it was done.

That is the power of the voice of God and the Word, Jesus Christ, who holds everything together in the universe. All of it is being held up by the power of His Word: "For by him were all things created, that are in heaven, and that are in earth, visible and invisible, whether they be thrones, or dominions, or principalities, or powers: all things were created by him, and for him: And he is before all things, and by him all things consist" (Colossians 1:16–17).

Also, "In the beginning was the Word, and the Word was with God, and the Word was God. The same was in the beginning with God. All things were made by him; and without him was not any thing made that was made. In him was life; and the life was the light of men. And the light shineth in darkness; and the darkness comprehended it not" (John 1:1–5).

And if God should ever withdraw His living, speaking Word from the universe, everything would collapse into chaos; all would return to vacuity and utter darkness.

The Father then sent His Son, the Living Word of God, into the world—the same Word whose power is holding together all of creation, yet here we find Him "wrapped in swaddling clothes and laid in a manger" (see Luke 2). And with the Word entering the world, because of His divine love and sacrifice at Calvary, two things we as human beings so desperately need were made possible: cleansing and quickening.

"Wherewithal shall a young man cleanse his way? by taking heed thereto according to thy word" (Psalm 119:9). You see, we need to be cleansed because we're so shamefully sinful and defiled. The Scripture here makes it clear that it is by His Word we are cleansed. We all need this cleansing by the Lord.

Not only is there cleansing in the Word, there's also quickening. The reason we need God's quickening is that we're morally and spiritually dead. We're dead with a deadness we ourselves can't bury. We're dead with a deadness that nobody can diagnose or cure. In the book of Psalms and elsewhere, the Scripture says it is He, Jesus Christ, who quickens us by His Word.

Notice how in the Bible, the Word of God and Jesus Christ the Word merge into one. The lyrics of William W. How's hymn testify to this blessed melding of the two:

O Word of God Incarnate

O Word of God incarnate,
O Wisdom from on high,
O Truth, unchanged, unchanging,
O Light of our dark sky,
we praise Thee for the radiance
that from the hallowed page,
a lantern to our footsteps,
shines on from age to age.

The writer seems almost confused, and it's the same sweet confusion a lover is confused with—someone deeply in love who is left in a state of happy wooziness. William How goes back and forth between talking about Jesus as the Word and the Word of God, the Bible.

There's a lot of confusion in the Scriptures, but not the kind that hurts you; it's the kind that edifies you. It's like a meadow, a forest, the blue sky above, or children at play. It's a confusion that blesses you.

We have in the Scriptures, then, Word and word, the first capitalized and the second not capitalized. "Which preach the word," said Paul, and we're not sure whether he meant "preach the Bible" or "preach Jesus" because the word is the book, and the word is flesh.

You have the Word made flesh walking around among us, and you have the word made into print to be bound and carried under your arm, to be loved, marked, wept and prayed over.

So we have the word and the Word, and you'll find that throughout the Bible, it's not completely clear whether the word means Christ, or whether it means the Bible, or whether it means both. It's perfectly all right to be confused by this. In fact, I'm suspicious of those who claim to know all the answers, especially as it pertains to God's Word. The happiest, most humble and honest thing we can say is, "I don't know."

In Psalm 119, it was God and David and the Word walking around together. God had tied David up in a bundle of life with the word and the Word, and that is where we still are today. There's no separating the living Word who speaks and the spoken word that is uttered by Him.

Here's where we must pull all this together. Our obedience to the Word is simply to surrender to the authority of God, allowing Him to direct our path. Nothing is more important than our obedience to the Lord because when we are obeying the Word of God, we're cooperating with the Holy Spirit in what He wishes to accomplish in us and through us. While we often don't have the slightest idea what the Holy Spirit is up to, it is our obedience to God that allows the Spirit to carry out His will in our lives.

Heavenly Father, sometimes I become confused concerning Your will in my life, and yet as I search Your Word, I begin to understand more little by little. I see that my obedience to You is not based on my understanding, but rather on Your command. Thank You for Your Word. In Jesus' name I pray, amen.

Thy Word Is Like a Garden, Lord

Your Word is like a garden, Lord,
with flowers bright and fair;
and everyone who seeks may pluck
a lovely cluster there.
Your Word is like a deep, deep mine;
and jewels rich and rare
are hidden in its mighty depths
for every searcher there.

Your Word is like a starry host;
a thousand rays of light
are seen to guide the traveler,
and make his pathway bright.
Your Word is like an armory,
where soldiers may repair,
and find, for life's long battle day,
all needful weapons there.

O may I love your precious Word,
may I explore the mine,
may I its fragrant flowers glean,
may light upon me shine.
O may I find my armor there,
your Word my trusty sword;
I'll learn to fight with every foe
the battle of the Lord.

Edwin Hodder

19

The Bible Energizes
Our Obedience

The law of thy mouth is better unto me than thousands
of gold and silver.

Psalm 119:72

David loved the Word of God. In the verse above, he was
talking about gold and silver because he'd been a soldier who
had gone out and captured a city, then searched through the
city's big houses to see how much spoil he could come away
with. He'd taken silver and gold and other valuable things.
He knew what it was like to capture a city and take the spoils,
but when he came to the Book of God, he found more spoil
than he'd found in all the cities of the world. "I rejoice at
thy word, as one that findeth great spoil" (Psalm 119:162).

In a more restrained mood, David said, "My soul hath kept
thy testimonies; and I love them exceedingly" (Psalm 119:167).

151

And David didn't have much of anything to read except the Pentateuch, while we have the Pentateuch plus the books of the prophets, the Proverbs, the Gospels, Paul's epistles, and Revelation, so in this way we're better off than he was. Yet David *loved* God's Word, exclaiming, "I rejoice in it exceedingly."

For it's in the Bible that we find Moses on the mountain, kneeling at the burning bush, covering his face, taking off his shoes, quaking and crying, "Holy, holy, holy" in the presence of God with His awesome wonder and unfathomable power.

Where else but in the Bible can we find Ezekiel—discouraged, gloomy, and alone—dabbling his feet in the swift-flowing water, a poor priest far from home (see Ezekiel 1:1–3). Then the heavens were opened, and he saw visions of God.

There's the story of Adam and Eve, of Noah and the ark, of Abraham and his son Isaac, of Moses and the Israelites crossing the Red Sea, of Daniel in the den of lions, of John the Baptist baptizing the Son of God, of Jesus' sacrifice at Calvary and His resurrection three days later, of the apostles gathered in the Upper Room in Jerusalem on the day of Pentecost, of Paul locked up in prison for preaching the gospel of the Living Christ, and of John the Evangelist on the Island of Patmos, receiving from God the vision of the seven seals, seven trumpets, and seven bowls. And on and on it goes. The Bible contains riches beyond measure—everything we need to know concerning the Triune God, divine love, faith, truth, redemption, communion, salvation, and prophecy.

If you're feeling discouraged, go with Elijah and stand on the mountaintop where he challenged the four hundred prophets of Baal. These prophets were standing around in their robes and with all their paraphernalia, and yet they hadn't been able to get a bit of fire going. Not a single flame.

Elijah said to them, "Maybe your god is on a journey, or maybe he's sleeping and needs to be woke up" (see 1 Kings 18:27). Elijah needled them all day long until they were so angry that if God hadn't answered Elijah's prayer, the prophets of Baal would likely have torn him limb from limb and thrown him from Mount Carmel. God had to answer. So when the sun set at the time of the evening sacrifice, Elijah poured the water around, got down on his knees, and earnestly prayed, "O Lord, send the fire."

Sure enough, God sent the fire, and the false prophets of Baal were completely defeated. Oh, what treasures we have in this Bible of ours.

The United States government once sent Benjamin Franklin to France as an ambassador. Once there, he was invited to a gathering of learned men, politicians, artists, poets, philosophers, and famous writers. During the evening, each of them would stand and read something aloud, and then everybody else would briefly comment on whether what they'd heard was good or not. If not, they would elaborate on what they thought was perhaps lacking in the writing.

When it was Franklin's turn to read something, he stood and read a short passage that took him about ten minutes, and then he sat down. This was followed by round after round of applause. "That," one of them said, "was better than anything we have heard read in years. Where, Mr. Franklin, did you get it? Did you write it yourself?"

Franklin replied, "That was from the book of Ruth—from the Bible."

And it was the most wonderful thing they had ever heard.

The Bible shows us the one pathway to salvation and eternal life with the Creator God, as salvation can be found only in the Word of God and nowhere else. After David confessed to his having gone astray like a lost sheep, he confirmed that it was the Lord God who brought him back again.

Go to the Bible, and it will speak living words to you that lead to immortality. I don't know about you, but I enjoy living. It would be a terrible shock if an angel were to come and tell me that I'd been mistaken and that when I died, that would be the end of me.

Consider for a moment the word *immortality*. The root word, *mort*, refers to death and therefore a *mortuary* is a place for those who are dead. And *mortal*, from the Latin *mortalis*, means deadly or subject to death. This is akin to the Latin *mori*, which is to die. Thus *immortal* means you are not subject to death; it means you will be in a state where you'll live on forever and ever.

Always check what others tell you against what you have learned in the Word of God, and if you can't find it there, turn your back on it. When you do, you will be turning your face to the Light. That is why we must base our obedience to God on the Bible. We can trust the Bible like no other book. And as we read and study God's Word, the Holy Spirit will enable us to understand its words and apply them to our daily lives.

Heavenly Father, when I discovered the Bible, I discovered You and everything I needed to learn more about You and to come to know Your Son as my Savior. I pray the Holy Spirit will continue to enrich my understanding of Your Word. In Jesus' name I pray, amen.

Savior, Like a Shepherd Lead Us

Savior, like a shepherd lead us,
Much we need Thy tender care;
In Thy pleasant pastures feed us,
For our use Thy folds prepare.
Blessed Jesus, blessed Jesus,
Thou hast bought us, Thine we are;
Blessed Jesus, blessed Jesus,
Thou hast bought us, Thine we are.

We are Thine, do Thou befriend us,
Be the guardian of our way;
Keep Thy flock, from sin defend us,
Seek us when we go astray:
Blessed Jesus, blessed Jesus,
Hear, O hear us when we pray;
Blessed Jesus, blessed Jesus,
Hear, O hear us when we pray.

Thou hast promised to receive us,
Poor and sinful though we be;
Thou hast mercy to relieve us,
Grace to cleanse, and pow'r to free:
Blessed Jesus, blessed Jesus,
Early let us turn to Thee;
Blessed Jesus, blessed Jesus,
Let us early turn to Thee.

Early let us seek Thy favor,
Early let us do Thy will;
Blessed Lord and only Savior,
With Thy love our bosoms fill:
Blessed Jesus, blessed Jesus,
Thou hast loved us, love us still;
Blessed Jesus, blessed Jesus,
Thou hast loved us, love us still.

Dorothy A. Thrupp

20

The Unity of Believers
through Obedience

*Behold, how good and how pleasant it is for brethren
to dwell together in unity! It is like the precious oint-
ment upon the head, that ran down upon the beard,
even Aaron's beard: that went down to the skirts of his
garments; As the dew of Hermon, and as the dew that
descended upon the mountains of Zion: for there the
Lord commanded the blessing, even life for evermore.*

Psalm 133:1–3

Here, painted by the pen of inspiration held by David, is one
of the most charming pictures presented in the entire Bible.
It is a picture of the brethren, and by *brethren* it does not
mean men only, but men, women, and young people, all of
them of the same mind, who meet together in unity. Because
they did meet together in unity, we read about such things
as oil, dew, life, and blessing.

The coming together in unity was man's part, whereas God's part was the pouring out of the oil, dew, life, blessing. As the rest of the Bible will attest, the Scripture above shows us that unity of mind on the part of the people of God precedes the blessing of God.

I have heard God's children pray a lot of prayers that never should have been prayed. I myself have prayed such prayers many times. But the Lord is ever gracious to us, for He edits our prayers and makes them acceptable.

The Holy Spirit, the Scripture says, knows what is the mind of God, and God knows the mind of the Spirit. He presents our prayers rightly so that what God hears is an edited prayer, which is a prayer He understands and amends for our sakes because He knows that which we do not.

One prayer I've heard that requires the Spirit's holy editing is, "O Lord, send the Holy Spirit so that we may become a united people." This gets things precisely backward. The Holy Spirit comes because we *are* a united people. He doesn't come to make us a united people. "Lord, come and bless us and unite us and help us to get united, so that your blessing might flow and there be an outpouring of life and wisdom from above." Now that's the way we should pray.

It says in the book of Acts, "When the day of Pentecost was fully come, they were all with one accord in one place. And suddenly there came a sound from heaven as of a rushing mighty wind, and it filled all the house where they were sitting. And there appeared unto them cloven tongues like as of fire, and it sat upon each of them. And they were all filled with the Holy Ghost, and began to speak with other tongues, as the Spirit gave them utterance" (Acts 2:1–4).

And so the disciples spoke with boldness, and the multitude believed and grew in size, and they were all of one heart and one soul: "All that believed were together, and had all things common; And sold their possessions and goods, and parted them to all men, as every man had need. And they, continuing daily with one accord in the temple, and breaking bread from house to house, did eat their meat with gladness and singleness of heart . . ." (Acts 2:44–46).

My assumption is that they had been like this all along. They didn't get unified because the place where they were assembled was suddenly shaken by the Spirit, and they were all filled. It doesn't say the multitude became of one heart; it says the multitude who believed were of one heart. There's an important difference.

And with great power, the apostles preached the Word, giving witness of the resurrection of the Lord Jesus, and the grace of God was upon them all. This teaches us that unity is necessary to have already in place in order for the outpouring of the Spirit of God to occur, to give His blessing among those gathered in Jesus' name.

Allow me to go to the scientific world for an illustration. If you have 120 volts of electricity coming into your house, but you have broken wiring or a blown fuse, you will not have power. You may flip a number of switches, but nothing lights up. The stove and the iron don't heat up. No radio or television comes on. You may have the power ready to be turned on to do its work, flowing to all the appliances you have in your home, but where there is broken wiring or a fuse that's blown, or because something else has come loose or is connected wrongly, you will have no power. None at all.

159

Unity, likewise, is absolutely necessary among the children of God—that is, if we are to know and experience the Spirit's flow of power and blessing.

The apostle Paul said, "If there be therefore any consolation in Christ, if any comfort of love, if any fellowship of the Spirit, if any bowels and mercies, fulfill ye my joy, that ye be like-minded, having the same love, being of one accord, of one mind. Let nothing be done through strife or vainglory; but in lowliness of mind let each esteem other better than themselves. Look not every man on his own things, but every man also on the things of others. Let this mind be in you, which was also in Christ Jesus . . ." (Philippians 2:1–5).

Whether big or small, revivals have mainly involved achieving oneness of mind amid a gathering of Christians. While there are many isolated blessings among God's people, revival is marked by the persistence of the spiritual mood and oneness. We all have times of spiritual moods, and there are occasional moments in churches when a sudden spiritual mood comes over the people of God gathered in one place. Revival, however, tends to carry over from day to day and from week to week. This persistence enables the Holy Spirit to do His holy work in us.

The average Christian attends church on Sunday, receives a little blessing, but then they lose it by Wednesday. It's a continual going up to the mountain peak, down into the valley, and back up to the peak again.

It's better to follow this path than none at all, but it's even better to stay there at a high level than to come down in midweek and have to run to a prayer meeting to climb back up. Weekly prayer meetings are fine and good, but we

160

should not have to go to one to mend our "broken wires." We ought to stay unified; we ought to be persisting. Our mood and spirituality ought to remain consistent.

Also, when I refer to a "oneness of mind," I am not referring to identical doctrinal views. It would be nearly impossible to achieve this. A Protestant church is not unlike a democratic society, and I believe the Christian Church as a whole ought to be akin to this kind of society. In a democratic society, people are free to have a variety of opinions, and usually do. But when the chips are down, they come together.

In the United States in 1941, there were divisions everywhere among our nation's people. It seemed every group was busy criticizing every other group that was different from their own. But when the Japanese bombed Pearl Harbor, this major event united the country overnight.

The news and tragedy of the bombing brought the people together, no matter their opposing views socially and politically. They were united until the war was over, and afterward they went back to slugging it out again. It's the same all over the world.

Nevertheless, there are in the Christian Church certain foundational truths that we stand for, that we believe are necessary to our spiritual lives as followers of the Lord. These great truths must be understood and affirmed or we don't have a Church. Therefore, we turn to the Apostles' Creed and the Nicene Creed, two of the most well-known creeds in the Church. They summarize the Bible's teachings and express the Christian's central beliefs.

For example, we believe in righteousness. We believe in the resurrection of the dead. We believe in the second coming of

Christ. We believe in the blood of the Lamb, Jesus Christ. We believe in the redeeming and cleansing power of that blood. We believe in the Lordship of Jesus. We believe in the Trinity. We believe in the reality of sin and its consequences. We believe in God's forgiveness.

Again, if we were to remove such beliefs from the Church, we would have no Church. Instead, we would have merely a religious organization and that's all. But if we incorporate these central beliefs into the life of the Church, teaching them and cultivating them, then we have a Church indeed, a fellowship of God's children.

And this is regardless of churches and individual Christians holding different views in other areas or doctrines, which of-tentimes are things that, when all is said and done, don't much matter.

So the oneness I'm talking about here is not the oneness of a totalitarian but of a democratic Church. If I preach something, and you search your Bible and find it isn't so, I don't want you to believe it. I want you to come to me and say, "Brother, I appreciated your sermon, but you were off in this one regard . . ." We all have the Bible, and it tests whether we're in the right or in the wrong.

All of this has much to do with our obedience to God's Word. Without God's Word, we have no basis for truth and nothing to be obedient to; rather, we would all be led by our own opinions and whims. As Christians we need to make God's Word the focal point of our fellowship in the Church, as well as our obedience to Jesus Christ.

Heavenly Father, send us the Holy Spirit so that we may become a united people for Your honor and glory. May we come together in unity around the Lord Jesus, our Savior and Redeemer. In Jesus' name we pray, amen.

And Can It Be, That I Should Gain?

And can it be that I should gain
An int'rest in the Savior's blood?
Died He for me, who caused His pain?
For me, who Him to death pursued?
Amazing love! how can it be
That Thou, my God, should die for me?

Amazing love! how can it be
That Thou, my God, should die for me!

'Tis mystery all! Th'Immortal dies!
Who can explore His strange design?
In vain the firstborn seraph tries
To sound the depths of love divine!
'Tis mercy all! let earth adore,
Let angel minds inquire no more.

He left His Father's throne above,
So free, so infinite His grace;
Emptied Himself of all but love,
And bled for Adam's helpless race;
'Tis mercy all, immense and free;
For, O my God, it found out me.

Long my imprisoned spirit lay
Fast bound in sin and nature's night;
Thine eye diffused a quick'ning ray,
I woke, the dungeon flamed with light;
My chains fell off, my heart was free;
I rose, went forth and followed Thee.

No condemnation now I dread;
Jesus, and all in Him is mine!
Alive in Him, my living Head,
And clothed in righteousness divine,
Bold I approach th'eternal throne,
And claim the crown, through Christ my own.

                                        Charles Wesley

21

Revival Empowered through Obedience

If my people, which are called by my name, shall humble themselves, and pray, and seek my face, and turn from their wicked ways; then will I hear from heaven, and will forgive their sin, and will heal their land.

2 Chronicles 7:14

One of the most important factors fueling a revival in any church is obedience. We must know what the Word of God says, we must understand how it applies to us, and we must seek to obey it with all of our hearts. Then, as we obey God's Word, He will begin to work through us in ways that will bless God and bring Him glory.

God will revive a church only if there's a oneness of determination to glorify Him. The Lord won't ask whether you are

Arminian or Calvinist, but He will ask, "Are you determined to glorify me alone?"

To realize this unity, God's people, the Church called by His name, are going to have to get together on this. We are not to honor people, though we may choose to honor those to whom honor is due in a secondary way, but we're to *glorify* the Lord only. We must never seek honor for ourselves. Instead, we should pray the words, "Glorify thyself, Lord," and pray them often. And He will surely bless those who are dedicated to the glorification of the Triune God.

Also, God will revive a church only if the people are united in their engrossment or preoccupation with the Lord's work and what it is He's doing in the world. This persistence of spiritual yearning in people is often interrupted by side interests and distractions.

God's will, however, is that His people remain wholly devoted to His Son, Jesus Christ, that they love the Word of God and His ways, and are committed to sacrificial obedience. I do not believe that God will continue to bless or send anything like a life-giving revival to a church until that church is dedicated to obedience to God and His Word.

We must also be united in our determination to see God perform His wonders. Let us cling to the words in the Gospel of Matthew, "Blessed are they which do hunger and thirst after righteousness: for they shall be filled" (Matthew 5:6). So says the mighty Word of God, and this is a promise that cannot be broken. If we thirst, therefore, we will be given living water to satisfy our thirst. If we hunger, we'll be fed to the point that our hunger will be assuaged by the Lord. This is the spiritual nourishment offered to us by the Lord out of His goodness.

God wants to do wonderful things for His people, to bless them and encourage them and heal them of their sicknesses, restoring them to health again. But first there has to be a unity of prayer for God's outpouring to be manifested. Praying is God's mysterious method of seeing that His will is carried out here on earth, and God has promised us that *all things are possible* for those who put their faith in Him.

Nothing, then, is impossible with God, and prayer is what unites God and the praying believer, and the Church as a whole. "Seeing then that we have a great high priest, that is passed into the heavens, Jesus the Son of God, let us hold fast our profession. For we have not an high priest which cannot be touched with the feeling of our infirmities; but was in all points tempted like as we are, yet without sin. *Let us therefore come boldly unto the throne of grace*, that we may obtain mercy, and find grace to help in time of need" (Hebrews 4:14–16, emphasis added).

And let's not forget Jesus' beautiful words: "Ask, and it shall be given you; seek, and ye shall find; knock, and it shall be opened unto you: For every one that asketh receiveth; and he that seeketh findeth; and to him that knocketh it shall be opened" (Matthew 7:7–8).

Asking and seeking and knocking require some degree of expectation. One of the greatest obstacles we can come across with our praying is to pray for vague things. When we pray in general terms, we're only shooting at the clouds. How would we know whether we have hit anything or not?

If we pray for something in specific terms, and God doesn't grant that something, it doesn't honor God for us to pretend as though we have it anyway. No, if someone, for instance, wishes to be filled with the Holy Spirit, they need to ask for this filling specifically, directly. We ought to be willing to allow God to test us and know whether our prayers have been answered or not.

Another requirement for revival is for the Church to be united in putting aside any public or private differences. If there are public differences, it is best that they be made right publicly; if there are private differences, they should be dealt with privately, but either way we must do everything we can to be one in Christ at all times.

Meanwhile, we must continue to be diligent in our walk with God: always prayerful, merciful, considerate of others, patient, and forgiving.

Living and worshiping together in unity among the people of God brings great blessing and spiritual anointing, which is a sign of the Lord's favor, protection, the outpouring of His mighty power. We must keep in mind that as Christians, we are all members of that body of which Jesus is the head.

Are we then in such a place where God can bless us? Are we in the pathway of obedience? Do we have this unity of determination to glorify the Lord alone? Do we share an engrossment with what He's doing as He works among us and on this earth in His mission of drawing the lost to himself? Do we have a unity of determination to see the Lord's wonders, as well as a submission to God to put aside anything that might hinder His blessings—His life and healing and grace—from flowing and being manifested?

I'd like to see every church so blessed and so anointed, much like how the spring makes the dull landscape come alive again with color and new life. We praise God for everything we have, and we thank Him for wonderful fellowship, but now it seems as if the Holy Spirit is saying, "Get thee up into the top of Pisgah, and lift up thine eyes westward, and northward, and southward, and eastward, and behold it with thine eyes: for thou shalt not go over this Jordan" (Deuteronomy 3:27).

I believe it's time we Christians determine together that we're going to seek out something new, something wonderful for our Church. And in order to be blessed with the revival God wants us to have, it all must begin with our united obedience to God's Word.

When the Holy Spirit moves, it's always within an atmosphere of humble obedience and unity among the people of God. We cannot be disobedient and also experience a move of God, just like Adam and Eve in the Garden of Eden lost their identity and connection with God because of their act of disobedience. It took only this one act of disobedience to bring havoc to all of humanity.

As we obey God, our thirst and hunger for Him will grow stronger and stronger. The more we come to know Him, the more we desire to obey Him. And the more we obey the Lord, the more we get to know Him. May this become a reality in Christian churches and congregations throughout the world, today and in the years to come.

Heavenly Father, I pray that my heart would desire more of Thee. I pray that, in obedience to Your Word, I may discover more about Thee each day that I live. In Jesus' name I pray, amen.

Revive Us Again

We praise thee, O God, for the Son of thy love,
for Jesus who died, and is now gone above.

Hallelujah! Thine the glory, hallelujah! Amen!
Hallelujah! Thine the glory, revive us again.

We praise thee, O God, for thy Spirit of light
who has shown us our Savior and scattered our night.

We praise thee, O God, for the joy thou hast giv'n
to thy saints in communion, these foretastes of heav'n.

Revive us again, fill each heart with thy love.
May each soul be rekindled with fire from above.

W. P. Mackay

A.W. TOZER QUOTES ON OBEDIENCE

From Tozer's book
The Crucified Life

"Obedience is a primary component of the Christian life."

"In looking at the lives of the men and women of the Old and New Testaments, and even throughout Church history, we find that it was obedience that often got them into difficulties."

"Dietrich Bonhoeffer's obedience sent him straight to the gallows. He could have escaped, but it would have required him to compromise his relationship to God, which was something he would never have thought of doing."

"True obedience is the refusal to compromise in any regard our relationship with God, regardless of the consequences."

"Obedience is recognizing God's sovereignty and authority and submitting to it without question and without regard to consequence."

From *The Pursuit of Man*

"When faith becomes obedience, then it is true faith indeed."

From *A Disruptive Faith*

"The heart that God uses is the heart yielded to Him in faith and obedience."

"Through the vehicle of obedience, the man or woman of faith will be led to that mysterious and wonderful place called the blessing of God."

From *Experiencing the Presence of God*

"I believe that *trust* and *obey* are like the two wings of a bird. A wise man once wrote, 'Two wings of a dove don't weigh her down. She rises by means of them.' Trust and obey are the two wings of the Christian. We trust, and we obey. We obey because we trust. We trust in order that we might obey. If we try to obey without faith, we get nowhere. If we try to have faith without obedience, it ends in nothing."

"Christ earned our trust and our obedience because He did not take the path of convenience, but went the way of the cross and died for us and became our great High Priest."

"Obedience is not something that comes naturally to any of us, particularly in the spiritual realm. There are many things arrayed against us, necessitating us to track all diligence in obeying the Scriptures."

"The key to disciplining ourselves in the area of obedience is always keeping in mind to whom we are being obedient."

From *Mystery of the Holy Spirit*

"But the Holy Spirit who inspired the Scriptures will expect obedience to the Scriptures. And if we do not obey the Scriptures, we will quench Him. He will have obedience, and people do not want to obey the Lord."

"The Spirit of God will not give a disobedient child His blessing. He will not fill a disobedient child with the Holy Spirit. There must be obedience there. Obedience to the Word, obedience to the Spirit, obedience to the risen Lord. You must be an obedient Christian. He gives His Holy Spirit to them that obey Him."

From *Rut, Rot, or Revival*

"Obedience to Christ proves we love Him, and in return He shows himself to us."

From *The Dangers of a Shallow Faith*

"That obedience to Jesus Christ, which Paul called slavery, is not the slavery that imposes itself from the outside by laws, nor by the introduction of alien ideas into the mind. It is the happy, joyous bondage of freedom and love, and the holiest and most free creature in heaven above is the angel that is nearest the throne of God."

From *The Wisdom of God*

"The obedient Christian will be the seeing Christian. It is by obedience that we take up the cross, not by singing about the cross. By taking up the cross we are obeying, and when we obey, we carry the cross. It is when the obedience of the cross comes into your life that you notice how wisdom and power are centered on the cross of Jesus Christ."

A.W. TOZER (1897–1963) was a self-taught theologian, pastor, and writer whose powerful words continue to grip the intellect and stir the soul of today's believer. He authored more than forty books. *The Pursuit of God* and *The Knowledge of the Holy* are considered modern devotional classics. Get Tozer information and quotes at X.com/TozerAW.

REVEREND JAMES L. SNYDER is an award-winning author and an authority on the life and ministry of A.W. Tozer. Because of his thorough knowledge of Tozer, James was given the rights from the A.W. Tozer estate to produce new books derived from over four hundred never-before-published audiotapes. He and his wife live in Ocala, Florida. Learn more at awtozerclassics.com, and connect with James at JamesSnyder51@gmail.com or at JamesSnyderMinistries.com.